Remembering Robert Laxalt

Conference Papers Series #22

Remembering Robert Laxalt

edited by

Iñaki Arrieta Baro, David Rio,
and Xabier Irujo

University of Nevada, Reno
Center for Basque Studies

With our gratitude for the generous support of the Government of Bizkaia.

Cover image courtesy of Marilyn Newton.

Center for Basque Studies
University of Nevada, Reno
1664 North Virginia St,
Reno, Nevada 89557 usa
http://basque.unr.edu

ISBN-13: 978-1-967179-10-7
EPUB ISBN: 978-1-967179-11-4

Library of Congress Cataloging-in-Publication Data
Names: Arrieta Baro, Iñaki, 1976- editor | Río, David editor | Irujo Ametzaga, Xabier editor
Title: Remembering Robert Laxalt / edited by Iñaki Arrieta Baro, David Rio, and Xabier Irujo.
Description: Reno : Center for Basque Studies Press, 2026. | Series: Conference papers series ; 22 | Includes bibliographical references and index. | Summary: "Commemorating the centennial of Robert Laxalt's birth, Remembering Robert Laxalt offers new perspectives on the writings of an author who may be regarded as the dean of Basque American literature and one of the most notable twentieth-century voices in Nevada and the American West"-- Provided by publisher.
Identifiers: LCCN 2026002759 (print) | LCCN 2026002760 (ebook) | ISBN 9781967179107 paperback | ISBN 9781967179114 epub
Subjects: LCSH: Laxalt, Robert, 1923-2001--Criticism and interpretation | Basque Americans | Basque American literature | LCGFT: Festschriften | Essays | Literary criticism
Classification: LCC PS3562.A9525 Z85 2026 (print) | LCC PS3562.A9525 (ebook)
LC record available at https://lccn.loc.gov/2026002759
LC ebook record available at https://lccn.loc.gov/2026002760

Printed in the United States of America

Contents

Introduction

by Iñaki Arrieta Baro, David Rio, and Xabier Irujo

In 2023, the Center for Basque Studies and the Jon Bilbao Basque Library of the University of Nevada, Reno, with the collaboration of the REWEST (Research in Western American Literature and Culture) group (EHU, University of the Basque Country) organized A Basque American Literary Pioneer: Robert Laxalt Centennial Conference (1923–2023). The events took place at the Mathewson-IGT Knowledge Center's rotunda on March 9–10, 2023.

The aim of the conference was to commemorate the centennial of Robert Laxalt's birth, offering new perspectives on the writings of an author who may be regarded as the dean of Basque American literature and one of the most notable twentieth-century voices in Nevada and the American West. Laxalt's literary career, consisting of seventeen books, is an authoritative reflection on the experiences of the Basques of his time both in the United States and in the Basque Country. The conference gathered seventeen scholars and writers from the United States and Europe. They explored topics related to Laxalt's writing and career, including his Basque American works, his literary representation of Nevada and the West, his journalistic pieces, his legacy at the University of Nevada, Reno, and his contribution to the cultural and social visibility of Basques in the US. All of which we have included in this book.

The Center for Basque Studies and the Basque Library had many reasons to organize a conference on Robert Laxalt.

The Center for Basque Studies is dedicated to promoting research, scholarship, and teaching related to Basque culture and history, while the Basque Library aims to preserve the memory of the Basque diaspora in the United States. Laxalt's work is an integral part of the Basque American literary canon, and a conference would provide a platform for scholars and writers to share their research and ideas on his work. A conference on Laxalt, known for his vivid descriptions of Basque culture and life in the American West. would help to bring attention to his work and keep his legacy alive.

However, Laxalt's work is also relevant to broader themes related to immigration, identity, and cultural preservation. His stories of Basque immigrants navigating life in the American West provided insights into the experiences of other immigrant groups and their contributions to American culture. As a writer, he explored the experiences of Basque immigrants and their struggles to maintain their cultural identity in a new and unfamiliar environment.

Laxalt's writing also reflects the diversity of American culture and serves to promote greater understanding and appreciation for different cultures and traditions. By sharing the stories of Basque immigrants and their unique experiences, Laxalt's work helps to broaden our understanding of the rich tapestry of cultures that make up American society. Moreover, his work can be seen as a form of cultural preservation because he sought to document the experiences of Basque immigrants and their contributions to American society. By preserving these stories and cultural traditions, Laxalt's work helps to ensure that they are not forgotten and can be passed down to future generations. Laxalt's work is not only important in the context of Basque American literature, but it also has broader implications for discussions of diversity, immigration, and cultural preservation. From this perspective, the conference on Laxalt also helped to foster connections between scholars, writers, and members of the Basque American community and served as a forum for discussion and collaboration on topics related to Basque American culture and history.

There is a proverb in Basque that reads, "We are because they were, and they will be because we are." This axiom encapsulates the idea of intergenerational continuity and the importance of preserving cultural heritage. "We are because they were" recognizes that our present-day existence is the result of the actions and sacrifices of our ancestors. They passed on their culture, traditions, and values to us, which have shaped our identity and sense of self. Our cultural heritage is, therefore, an integral part of who we are, and we must acknowledge and honor the contributions of those who came before us. "They will be because we are" emphasizes the responsibility that we have to preserve our cultural heritage and pass it on to future generations. Just as our ancestors passed on their culture to us, it is our duty to ensure that our cultural traditions and values are preserved and passed on to future generations. By doing so, we ensure that our cultural heritage continues to thrive and evolve and that our descendants can continue to identify with and be proud of their cultural heritage.

Culture is the soil in which science, economy, and social development grow. Culture is the set of beliefs, values, customs, and behaviors that define a society. It shapes the way people think and behave and influences their interactions with others. In this sense, culture provides the context and framework within which scientific, economic, and social development takes place. Scientific development relies on a culture of curiosity, experimentation, and innovation. It requires a society that values knowledge, critical thinking, and open-mindedness. Economic development, on the other hand, depends on a culture of entrepreneurship, risk-taking, and investment. It requires a society that values hard work, creativity, and cooperation. Similarly, social development depends on a culture of inclusivity, compassion, and social justice. It requires a society that values human rights, equality, and the well-being of all its members.

Laxalt's accomplishments and his writings show that societies need to promote cultural growth that is inclusive, equitable, and promotes social justice while also recognizing the importance of cultural diversity and preserving the unique cultural traditions of different communities.

The first essay in the volume is aptly written by Robert Laxalt's older daughter, Monique Laxalt, a distinguished Nevada lawyer and the author of the semiautobiographical novel *The Deep Blue Memory*, who offers an insightful and personal summary of some of the most remarkable events in her father's life and literary career. Monique Laxalt's essay not only highlights her father's love for Nevada and the Basque Country but also addresses the complexity hidden behind the apparent simplicity of Laxalt's best-known book, *Sweet Promised Land.* Above all, this essay reveals her father's most significant literary gift, "the ability to write honestly and straightforwardly, but also poetically, from the heart."

After Monique Laxalt's opening essay, several chapters by scholars and other writers focus on different subjects related to Robert Laxalt's life and works, emphasizing his writing career. The author of the second essay, Warren Lerude, a veteran journalist and Laxalt's longtime friend and colleague at the University of Nevada, Reno, traces Laxalt's path to literature through journalism. He describes both his reporter days for United Press and his work in magazine journalism, including his articles for *National Geographic.* Lerude also points to the success of Laxalt as a professor at the Reynolds School of Journalism, in particular, because of his seminar "From Journalism to Literature," where he emphasized human character and writer detachment while his students analyzed some of the major books by authors such as Ernest Hemingway, John Steinbeck, Stephen Crane, and Jack London.

The following two essays focus on Laxalt's most iconic book, his impressive memoir, and biography of his father, Dominique, *Sweet Promised Land.* Xabier Irujo, the current director of the Center for Basque Studies at the University of Nevada, Reno, explores the way in which *Sweet Promised Land* enables its readers to discover Laxalt's Basqueness and gain a proper understanding of Basque identity and culture. Irujo also argues that Laxalt, in this memoir, "by exploring the complexities of identity and belonging through the lens of his own experiences and heritage, invites readers to reflect on their own sense of identity and the forces that shape it."

The second essay on *Sweet Promised Land* is written by two other Center for Basque Studies faculty members, Sandra Ott and Mariann Vaczi, who both teach Laxalt's highly acclaimed memoir in their online and in-person courses on Basque culture. The essay discusses the book's reception by American college students through students' critical receptions about their own homeland as a promised land, Basque immigrant experiences in the past, and comparisons with immigrant experiences today. Both authors emphasize the role of *Sweet Promised Land* as an excellent teaching tool to reflect on the myths and realities of immigration across generations.

Laxalt's Basque family trilogy, consisting of the novels *The Basque Hotel*, *Child of the Holy Ghost*, and *The Governor's Mansion*, is the subject of the next chapter. In this chapter, David Rio, the author of the first critical study on Laxalt's literary career (*Robert Laxalt: The Voice of the Basques in American Literature*), explores the interaction between place and identity in his Basque family trilogy. It is argued that in these novels the main characters' subjective perceptions of geographical space play a key role in the construction of their identities. Particular attention is paid to the symbolic meaning of iconic places in this trilogy, such as the Basque hotel in Carson City, the family house in the Basque Country or the Governor's Mansion, emphasizing their connection to the main characters' ethnic identity and to their integration process into American society. The trilogy also works as an insightful tool to approach issues such as rootedness, adjustment, alienation, dislocation, and nostalgia, and their relationship with the immigration experience.

After these chapters focus on some of the best-known books by Laxalt, this book charts the ways in which his work has influenced other western writers and scholars, and even social events.

Basque American and Nevada author, Gretchen Skivington, whose novel *Echevarria* was greatly influenced by the American Basque themes of Laxalt's works, wrote a chapter exploring Laxalt's impact on present-day authors and scholars. Skivington offers a compilation of the views of several western men and women (most of them related to the writing world and the academia) that illustrate the far-reaching impact of Laxalt's life and career. Among the authors who in Skivington's piece acknowledge Laxalt's powerful influence on their own literary careers are Frank Bergon, Shaun Griffin, Hank Nuwer, and Skivington herself. to name just a few contemporary writers deeply connected to Nevada.

The next chapter addresses the legacy of Laxalt's life and career beyond the literary field, examining issues such as his contribution to the cultural and social visibility of Basque Americans in the West and his legacy at the University of Nevada, Reno. Monika Madinabeitia, a Basque professor at Mondragon University and the author of the illustrated book *Petra, My Basque Grandmother*, examines the creation of what came to be known as the First Western Basque Festival in 1959, its goals, accomplishments, and its aftermath by emphasizing Laxalt's involvement in it. As Laxalt himself wrote for the festival tabloid, this event was "designed both as a funfest and as a tribute" to the Basque people, "about whom so little is known in this country. It will mark the first major interstate gathering of Basques, their families, and friends from all parts of the West."

William A. Douglass, the founder and director of the Basque Studies Program (now known as the William A. Douglass Center for Basque Studies) at the University of Nevada, Reno, is the author of the next piece in the volume, a very personal approach to his close relationship with Laxalt since 1963. Douglass explores the way in which Laxalt's career and his own configured one another for almost fifty years, enabling the readers to learn about Laxalt's contribution to the birth of the Basque Studies Program in 1967, his connection with this program under Douglass's direction, and his role in the creation of the Basque Book Series within the University of Nevada Press.

The book ends with an epilogue by Gabriel Urza, Robert Laxalt's grandson and the author of the novella *The White Death: An Illusion,* and the novels *All That Followed* and *The Silver State*. It is certainly a proper ending for this book because his chapter allows readers to gain a deeper understanding of Laxalt's personal and literary legacy. After all, this Basque American literary pioneer has become a reference for a new generation of authors who, through Laxalt's work, are able to develop an insightful perspective of themselves and their cultural heritage. Laxalt's torch has certainly been passed to new voices who have learned from the sheepherder's son the gift of writing from the heart.

The Soul of a Writer

On the Occasion of the One Hundredth Birthday of my Father, Robert Laxalt

by Monique Laxalt

On my own behalf and on behalf of my sister, Kristin, my children, Gabriel and Alexandra, Kristin's children, Amy and Kevin, and our children's children, I would like to extend our gratitude to the William A. Douglass Center for Basque Studies, to the University of Nevada, Reno, to the University of the Basque Country, and to all those who have invested so much in putting together this event honoring our father, grandfather, and great-grandfather, Robert Laxalt, on the occasion of his one hundredth birthday.

Part One: Before *Sweet Promised Land*

My father, Robert Laxalt, came into this world one hundred years ago, in 1923, the second of six children of Basque immigrants Dominique and Theresa Laxalt.

Robert was born in a small medical clinic in Alturas, California, close to the sheep camp where his father was running sheep and his mother cooking in a sheep tent over a wood stove. By the time Robert was four, the family had saved enough to settle in Carson City, the capital of Nevada, where they bought into a restaurant-boarding house where Theresa would cook, Dominique would tend bar, and a hired girl would help tend to the children.

The children's first language was Basque. Then, as the children started school, they would become fluent in English.

When Robert was about eight years old, he fell ill with rheumatic fever and was required to lie in bed for a year. During this time his mother and siblings would come and go from the Carson City Library with books for him to read. That early experience instilled in him a love of the written word and of written stories, and it developed in him a strong curiosity about the characters and experiences of Nevada's people. He began to write stories himself, his long illness having given him a quiet but relentless determination.

All this contributed to the formation of a young man who would as a young adult initially take the road of telling stories through journalism, as professor Warren Lerude will describe in his wonderful talk today (a later chapter). Journalism taught Robert to write the kind of short, clean sentences that would come to characterize his writing.

But in my own mind, his most important gift, the gift that so often sets apart the true writer—was the ability to write honestly and straightforwardly, but also poetically, from the heart.

While still in his twenties, during his early years as a journalist, my father married our mother, Joyce Nielsen, a beautiful towheaded young woman of Scandinavian descent.

Upon their marriage in Reno in 1949, Robert and Joyce settled first in a small apartment in Reno, so that Robert could have the independence he needed from the burgeoning extended family in Carson City. Soon thereafter, expecting their first child, they moved into a two-bedroom house in Reno. By this time Dominique and Theresa had moved out of the hotel-boarding house on Main Street in Carson, having saved enough to make a down payment on a white-washed house on Minnesota Street, one of the quiet, cottonwood-lined backstreets of Carson.

Dominique soon resumed sheepherding, much to his happiness in being back out in the hills and on the desert. He took job after job tending sheep in the high mountains in summer, and at desert ranches in winter. He was gone so much that my father's mother was known to declare that "a man like him should never have married."

And so if my parents wanted to spend time with Robert's father, it would have to be at one of his camps.

Even before the birth of their first child, Robert and Joyce would make regular visits to Dominique at his sheep camps in the mountains.

They each were enamored not only of Dominique but of the rustic settings of the camps, which my father had known and loved since childhood. Inevitably my parents would bring cheese and salami, and our grandfather would provide a loaf of bread he had baked himself in an oven made of rocks. And always the bota bag, filled with red wine.

Then came their first child, a towheaded little boy named Bruce, who was still a toddler as he tried to run after his grandfather's sheep in the high mountains. In later years, when the three of us were still young children, our parents would take us up to our grandfather's summer camp and leave us with him for several days. At night, he would bundle us into bedding he had laid out on the floor of the canvas tent, and in the morning we would wake to the amazing smell of bacon and fried eggs sizzling over the fire in an iron skillet.

Through countless visits to our grandfather's camps in Nevada's mountains and deserts, our father and mother instilled in us a deep connection to Nevada's land and to the sheepherder who was our grandfather, a connection that would be passed down to our own children and grandchildren.

Part Two: *Sweet Promised Land*

Then, in 1953, our father's life took a different turn, one that would forever change him and set the trajectory of his writing career.

With the encouragement of his siblings, Robert—now age thirty, married, with one child and a second on the way—convinced his father to go with him on a journey to Dominique's homeland, and the deep-green mountains of the Basque Country. Dominique had not returned since his departure, at age sixteen in 1906.

To put it mildly, my father was stunned by the beauty of the Basque Country and its people, and by the love with which both Dominique and his son were greeted. Once they arrived in the mountain village of Tardets the village in which Dominique had grown up, each night at dinner his sisters, now old, would ask Dominique question after question. They asked about his decades in America and about the time when his prosperous stock operations had crashed and he had stopped writing home. As my father would later tell me, it was during the late-night hours when the farmhouse was still that my father would curl up in his bed with a notepad and write note after note of what he had seen, and what he had heard, that day. My father, during the day, kept with him his 8 mm movie camera, which allowed him to capture memorable images. One example is Dominique's visit to the Tardets cemetery, where so many members of his family, and so many friends from youth, were buried.

From the moment of their return, and for years thereafter, the background music in our house in Reno would be the sound that came from my father's black Royal typewriter that our father's mother had given him as a teenager. The music of the typewriter was there as we slept at night, on weekends as we played. The sound of the typewriter became more and more pronounced as each month passed after our father's and grandfather's return home to Nevada.

Each evening after my father came home from his work as a young journalist by day, my parents would sit on our living room couch and sip cocktails and our mother read what our father had written during the night and early morning hours and would make comments and give suggestions.

And then one afternoon when we children were six and four and two, my father came home early from his work at the university, and my parents sat us on the front step of our little house and poured champagne for each of us. The words "Harper & Brothers" and "New York agent" and "contract" were fused in our minds with the taste of the champagne and the warmth of the afternoon.

And then some time after that, my father handed each of us a book that was dark blue, had form and shape and weight. It was *Sweet Promised Land,* each copy individually inscribed.

I have retrieved my own copy from my shelf of my father's books. His inscription to me reads as follows:

> To my Monique—
>
> By the time you can understand this, you will remember little of your grandfather. But this may in some part show you what kind of a man he was.
>
> Your father—
>
> Robert Laxalt

When I was older and was able to read and understand, I came to know that my father had spent one full year at his Royal typewriter and discarded innumerable sheets of paper before being struck by the clean, simple opening to the book: "My father was a sheepherder, and his home was the hills. So it began when he was a boy in the misted Pyrenees of France, and so it was to be for the most of his lifetime in the lonely Sierra of Nevada."

And I came to understand the heartbreaking final passage, describing Dominique's and Robert's departure after saying their final goodbyes:

> When, finally, we had made our way out of the house and were descending the sheep trail, with the song of good-by following after us, someone began to call. "Come back! Come back!"
>
> I looked at my father, but he did not even seem to have heard. His face was white and grim and violently disturbed, and he was breathing in quick gasps. I reached out and touched him on the arm and said uncertainly, "They want us to come back."
>
> Without turning, he shook his head and cried shakenly, "I can't go back. It ain't my country anymore. I've lived too much in America ever to go back." And then, angrily, "Don't you know that?"
>
> And suddenly before me, I saw the West rising up at dawn with an awesome vastness of deserts and mighty mountain ranges. I saw a band of sheep wending their way down a lonely mountain ravine of sagebrush and pine, and I smelled their dust and heard their muted bleating and the lovely tinkle of their bells. I saw a man in crude garb with a walking stick following after with his dog, and once he paused to mark the way of the land. Then I saw a cragged face that that land had had filled with hope and torn with pain, had changed from young to old, and in the end had claimed. And then, I did know it.
>
> We walked in silence down the wooded trail, and in a little while the voices died away.

Then later, when we were able to even better understand the book my father had given us, I realized, first, the complexity of a book that seemed to have been written with such simplicity. The book, I saw, contained the story of so many young Basque sheepherders who had grown old in the new land.

But I also realized that the book *Sweet Promised Land* was at the same time the story of my father's first discovery of the gentle beauty of his ancestral land and its people, and of his own strong connection to them. So much so that he and our mother and we three children, would, on two separate occasions while we were still children, spend an entire year living in a Basque village while our father wrote.

In one of the books he wrote in the Basque Country, *In a Hundred Graves*, my father described his walks "through a hundred graveyards in this tiny land . . . reading the lineage of a hundred villages."

Then he wrote:

> A thousand generations of my ancestors have gone down into this ground. Sometimes when I walk through the aisles of stone, the smell of the ground rises up. It is old and familiar, and I know instantly that this ground is in me.
>
> I have been buried here in a hundred little graveyards.

I believe that from that point forward he would love his Nevada and his Basque Country equally, and that his writing would be gifts to each.

Robert Laxalt

From Deadline Journalist to Acclaimed Author

by Warren Lerude

Robert Laxalt set his path toward literature through journalism as a reporter for the internationally competitive United Press wire service. He covered the drama of breaking news—a sawed-off shotgun mob assassination in a dark Reno alley, a million-dollar burglary in the secretive basement of a mysterious stone mansion, the execution of a smiling nineteen-year-old killer in the Nevada State Prison gas chamber. As a reporter, he faced deadlines every minute.[1]

Laxalt studied—and eventually taught—how journalism was intertwined with literature in the lives of Ernest Hemingway, John Steinbeck, Stephen Crane, and others who started out as journalists and developed their disciplined styles as authors.

Laxalt did the same. He shifted to and from book authorship to magazine journalism writing about world cultures, including the Basque people, for *National Geographic*. He created the University of Nevada Press to enable others, including academics, to become authors. And he helped develop the Reynolds School of Journalism as a distinguished author. The Reynolds

School created the Robert Laxalt Distinguished Writer Program as a memorial, inviting acclaimed journalist/authors to share expertise with students and the public each year.

Laxalt was drawn to storytelling as a young boy confined to his bed with life-threatening rheumatic fever in his Cason City, Nevada, home. Family and friends brought him books from the state library. As other children played games beyond his isolated window, he read books—Edgar Rice Burrough's *Tarzan of the Apes*, Albert Payson Terhune's *Sunnybank*, Jack London's Yukon stories, and many others. The books fired his imagination.

"I developed an insatiable appetite for all these treasures," he would one day write in an essay entitled "The Library and I."

"Even in summers when I went to the desert and mountain sheep camps of my father, Nevada State Library books went with me." When he returned the books, they carried the scent and aroma of sagebrush, and as he recalled, ". . . underwent a thorough airing before they were put back on the shelves." Laxalt credited the state library as a legacy for the love of writing that would become the consuming passion of his life.[2]

Recovering from illness, he won early acclaim in elementary school journalism as editor of *The Sixth Grade Chatter.* The little mimeographed newspaper had a big prediction: "We believe that if Robert Laxalt, our editor in chief, continues his efforts as a writer, he will some day make a name for himself in the literary world." He continued to read a book each day, picking one up and dropping another off at the library on his way to and from school.

In high school, Laxalt learned what he called the "pure love of language." English teacher Grace Bordewich recited poetry and conveyed images through the power of words. She inspired bringing prose to life as she assigned students short stories to write. He wrote about a detective and hoped for the best when he turned it in the next day. The teacher praised his story and read it aloud to the class. The recognition encouraged him.[3]

Laxalt attended Santa Clara University following his graduation in 1940. He volunteered for service when World War II broke out in 1941 and served as a code officer in Africa's spy-infested Congo. Stricken with malaria, he was sent home to heal. He enrolled at the University of Nevada in Reno in 1945 at age twenty-one. He studied literature not journalism, figuring he could learn the latter writing part-time for the Reno newspapers. He wrote sports for the *Nevada State Journal* and covered Carson City, the state capital, for both morning and evening newspapers.

Laxalt's creativity would be matched for life when he met pretty, blond coed Joyce Winfred Nielsen. She had been an actress during her four years at Reno High School and graduated at age sixteen to enroll at the university and study English literature and French. She was a fourth-generation Nevadan of Nordic descent whose mother and grandmother had graduated from the university and become teachers.

Joyce Nielsen was in sharp contrast to Laxalt, a first-generation Nevadan from a French Basque family that had no previous university education. Their campus courtship followed, and their interests bonded in his writing and her theater and creative analysis and continued after college and throughout their marriage.[4]

Laxalt began his full-time professional career as a journalist when he opened his own news operation in 1947 at age twenty-four.

Reno's morning newspaper reported: "Items appearing in the *Nevada State Journal* and bearing the credit initials, CNS, are disseminated by the Capitol News Service, which will begin full-scale operations in Carson City Monday.[5]

"The news agency is being founded by Robert Laxalt, well-known Carson City resident, who has been one of the

Journal's Carson City correspondents for many months." Laxalt covered everything he found interesting. The headlines declared the news, but Laxalt's prose enriched the stories.

Nevada Athlete Proposes Boxing as School Sport

by Robert Laxalt, Capitol News Service

Carson City, Nevada. "From days of old when gladiators bound their hands with metal strips and went forth to pound each other's faces into bleeding pulp, the manly art of boxing has often been proclaimed as the nearest throwback to barbarism that any age could offer. . . ."

Laxalt covered news of crime and tragedy, government, politics, and finance. He wrote feature stories about people of character, or lack of it, the celebrated and the notorious.

Laxalt developed his writing style in these early journalist days.

Spirit of the West

"In the days when Nevada was a wide expanse of frontier . . . the early settlers carved out of the wilderness a civilization founded on the principles of fortitude. . . ."

This kind of writing by Laxalt drew the attention of the United Press (UP) wire service bureau in Reno. Two years out of college, his Capitol News Service a success, he signed on as a staff correspondent with UP which began to dispatch his reporting nationally.

Dateline—Carson City, Nevada, April 23, 1949

By Robert Laxalt, United Press Correspondent

"David Blackwell, teen-age killer of two Reno policemen, died with a smile on his face at dawn yesterday.

"The 19 year old former high school student . . . was strapped into the execution chair in the gas chamber at the

Nevada State Prison at 5:14 a.m.

"At 5:17 a.m., the hydrocyanic fumes were released and five seconds later he was unconscious.

"Breathing stopped at 5:22 a.m. and at 5:26 a.m., nine minutes after the cyanide tablets tumbled into the vat of sulphuric acid beneath the chair, Blackwell was pronounced dead.

"Blackwell had a final visit with his parents and brother yesterday afternoon. He was calm and outwardly cheerful during the farewell scene, and, when one minister said goodbye, Blackwell answered, "It's not goodbye—it's so long."

Laxalt covered more executions as part of his job as a reporter but reached his limit when one went badly. "It just took too long to die," he said after the botched execution. He asked the United Press to assign another reporter in the future.[6]

Laxalt covered the intrigues of Reno's infamous open gambling and easy divorce laws including scandals. The Reno dateline was hot, and it got hotter November 18, 1949, with the headline *Wounded Gambler Fights for Life.*

Laxalt covered the attempted assassination of Lincoln Fitzgerald, owner of the Nevada Club casino, by assailants' sawed-off shotgun at close range in the driveway of his expensive home in southwest Reno. Fitzgerald survived with severe injuries. Investigators tied the legal Reno gambler to earlier illegal gambling in Michigan and suspected mobsters from Detroit ordered the trigger to be pulled.

Laxalt developed as a veteran reporter covering the February 29, 1952, $2,500,000 burglary of a reclusive multimillionaire. LaVere Redfield, a financier and land speculator, had hoarded a fortune, much of it in silver dollars, in the secret basement of his stone mansion. A frequent dinner companion, Marie D'Arc Michaud, a blue-eyed French Canadian songwriter, was suspected of working with a pack of thieves. The story made international headlines.

Laxalt saw potential in the longer form of magazine journalism. He had written several articles for *The American Weekly*, a Hearst Sunday newspaper supplement. He pitched the story of the eccentric Redfield to editor Charles Robbins in New York. Laxalt explained to the editor he had earned Redfield's trust while covering his story.[7]

The magazine headlined: *Down to His Last Million*

Laxalt's style as a suspense writer read like fiction but was as factual as his United Press news stories had been.[8]

> For years the forbidding house on the hill had been a source of curiosity to residents of Reno.
>
> Its high towers, its shadowed grounds, its barrier of high walls were in sharp contrast to the white frame houses surrounding it.
>
> People called it the "house on the hill" and wondered idly why its occupants were never about.

Laxalt knew how to paint a picture with words about the "man in blue jeans and shapeless hat. . . . with his dog, a Kerry Blue terrier . . . wandering around the grounds as though he was the gander . . ." He enticed the reader: "What manner of man was this who kept millions hidden in a bedroom closet, who left his house untended and his money ungraded, who could honestly say that he would rather lose $3,000,000 anytime than lose his dog?"

Laxalt answered the questions in narrative detail and provided both Redfield and the reader a soft and kind ending. He reported that the one-time recluse who had become notorious had one wish: "All he desires now is that people understand him as a man—not a multi-millionaire."

Laxalt continued to write a string of feature articles for *The American Weekly* as well as breaking news stories for United

Press and dozens of financial and western culture stories as the Nevada stringer (freelance correspondent) for *The Wall Street Journal*. He broke into major magazine writing with a piece in *The Saturday Evening Post* on September 20, 1952, entitled "What Has Wide-Open Gambling Done to Nevada?" And he had been thinking of publishing his first book from a collection of columns he had written for the *Nevada State Journal*. It would be entitled *The Violent Land, Tales The Old Timers Tell About Nevada*.[9]

The content lived up to the title. Laxalt selected items from hundreds of columns he had written for the *Nevada State Journal*: "Mercy and the Soldier," "Black Wallace," "The Cursed Mine," "The Lieutenant's Uncertainty," The Gentleman Leaves Town," "Sam Brown's Humiliation," "The Horse Traders."

The book was published in 1953 by the Nevada Publishing Company with typography and lithography by Silver State Press in Reno and illustrated by Richard Allen. It ran sixty-eight softbound pages with twelve stories.

Laxalt captured the reader's interest in the first paragraph of "Mercy and the Soldier":

> The private's face was rigid and expressionless, but there were deep flushes of red about his eyes.
>
> Before him raged the hulking figure of Sergeant Anton Kelly.

The second paragraph held the reader:

> "You're soft, Newton," the sergeant cried in his low, bull voice. "You're as soft inside as a woman. But I'm going to take it out of you. I'm going to take it out of you if it's the last thing I do."

Laxalt's journalistic short sentences, active verbs, dramatic detail, and a punchy ending evolved into the prose of authorship as the private killed the sergeant with a crack shot and escaped.

Laxalt signed the first copy in black ink on the tan paper of the book's title page.

> July 1, 1953
>
> Dear Mom-
>
> In thanks for all you did for me—so that something like this could be possible.

The Violent Land became one of seventeen books Laxalt would write in a career balancing between journalism, literature, and publishing. After five years with United Press, the wire service considered him a veteran reporter and asked him to move from Reno to larger bureaus, perhaps Los Angeles or Mexico City. But he knew he belonged in the mountain West. He resigned from UP and, when no other journalism jobs were available locally, he looked for a compatible position he learned might be created soon in a public information office for the University of Nevada.

The lull between jobs afforded him an opportunity to explore his own family roots and to think about another story, perhaps a magazine article, maybe even a book. It would be about Laxalt accompanying his father, Dominique, a veteran sheepherder in the isolated deserts and mountains of Nevada and California, on a visit to the Basque Country of France where he had been born sixty-six years earlier.

The family had been plotting to have Dominique return to the Basque Country because he frequently talked about going to see family and friends he had left behind when he came to America. It would, however, take considerable family planning—and persuasion—to have him actually do it.

Laxalt accompanied his father and made notes as they visited the old villages with their slate roofs and the church in the town square where he had played handball in his youth. Laxalt noted how his father's sisters, whom he had not seen in more than four decades, and others, celebrated what amounted to Dominique's triumph establishing himself in America.

Laxalt's journalistic instincts told him there was a good story in Dominique's discovery that, in fact, his home was no longer the Basque Country of his birth but the America he had found in Carson City and the nearby Sierra Nevada.

But what kind of story? He contacted an agent he knew in New York who suggested he write it as a book. But that posed a problem. He didn't know how to write it. Would it be a biography of Dominique? An autobiography of Laxalt himself? A memoir of each? Maybe a novel? And how could he even begin such a book? He put paper in his typewriter and tried repeatedly. He wrote words that didn't work. They weren't good enough. He tossed the paper from his typewriter into a wastebasket. Finally, he wrote, "My father was a sheepherder, and his home was the hills."[10]

Sweet Promised Land was published by Harper & Brothers in 1957 and won national acclaim:

Miami Herald—"Laxalt speaks not only for Basques, but for the Italians and Yugoslavs, for the Swedes and the Irish, the Portuguese and the Greeks—all our second-generation citizens. Rarely have they had a more eloquent spokesman."

The New York Times—"(The) book deserves universal regard as a classic of Americana."

The Washington Post—"An example of the art of writing."[11]

Sweet Promised Land established Laxalt as an author and provided him the credibility needed to establish the University of Nevada Press four years later. As he took on the challenges of publishing books by other authors, he continued to write his own, including a novel, *A Man in the Wheatfield,* in 1964.

Publisher Harper & Row described it as a "stark and chilling parable for our day . . . that . . . speaks of the corroding fears and prejudices that are the age-old foes of innocence, and separate man from his fellow man." *Time* magazine called it "a fascinating, ambiguous allegory of man's various says of confronting fear." Others compared it to Hemingway's *The Old Man and the Sea.*"[12]

The acclaim of *Sweet Promised Land* and *A Man in the Wheatfield* shifted Laxalt's attention to magazine journalism at the highest level. *National Geographic* published deeply researched and carefully written articles about the diverse cultures of the world. Laxalt thought he had one, a story about Basques.

Basque Sheepherders: Lonely Sentinels of the American West was published in June 1966 in the magazine priced at one dollar a copy or eight dollars for a year's subscription. The eighteen-page article was accompanied by twenty color photographs by William Belknap Jr., including one of Dominique with his iron-gray hair and Laxalt in the wide brimmed hat of seasoned cowboys.

Laxalt wrote closer to home with a piece published in June 1974 entitled "The Other Nevada" which he opened, "When I'm in Virginia City, I visit Gordon Lane, the genial owner of the Union Brewery Saloon." He and photographer J. Bruce Baumann then took the readers on a twenty-one-page jaunt through the Nevada snowy deserts and neon-lit cities, galloping wild horses, broken-down buckeroos, millionaire yachtsmen, and women jockeys in an ostrich race through city streets . . .

Laxalt turned again to his ethnic culture for *National Geographic* that same year in the December 1974 issue for an article entitled "The Enduring Pyrenees." He traveled to the Basque Country with photographer Edwin Stuart Grosvenor whose close-up images accompanied Laxalt's descriptions of the sturdy people, their stone houses in ancient villages, and cascading waterfalls plunging into green valleys from jagged peaks.

Laxalt's string of *National Geographic* articles continued for nineteen years through the 1985 issue with an article entitled "16th Century Basque Whaling in America." At the same time he wrote two books, *Nevada: A History* (1977) and *Nevada: A Bicentennial History (States and the Nation)* (1977). Others followed, including the fictional *A Cup of Tea in Pamplona* (1985), which was considered for a Pulitzer Prize and a semi-fictional trilogy about the Laxalt family, *The Basque Hotel* (1989), *Child of the Holy Ghost* (1992), and *The Governor's Mansion* (1994).

Laxalt's skills in journalism and literature as well as his extensive knowledge in publishing were coveted by the Reynolds School of Journalism on the Reno campus when he retired in 1983 from his directorship at the University of Nevada Press he had founded twenty-two years earlier. It was well established with a team of editors, scholars, and administrators he had put in place. And, at sixty, he wanted to take more time for his own writing.

A journalistic colleague and longtime friend, this writer, suggested he share his talent with students at the journalism school. Laxalt's career had developed to the highest levels of international journalism and global literary acclaim. So, it was natural for him to teach what he knew. He collaborated with the dean and faculty to arrange two classes, magazine journalism in the fall semester and literary journalism in the spring.

In the magazine class, Laxalt explained what he called "the most demanding writing one could ask for," the "rules and regulations" of *National Geographic.*

"First," he told the students in a way both serious and lighthearted, "let me explain Mother Geo's process . . . They sent me 5,000 words of instructions on how to write a 5,000-word story!" He went into the exacting detail of researching articles, spending up to six weeks developing sources and traveling to places such as Argentina to write about the gauchos. Then, he explained, it took another month to organize his notes and write a first draft. After that, he worked with up to six editors with their "disseminating comments."

Laxalt said he then had two choices—assimilating their comments into a second draft or "fight a feisty battle as to why they wouldn't work."[13]

Laxalt provided the magazine students with a detailed, twelve-page outline that included an introduction of himself as both professor and moderator of their own work. He worked from carefully prepared notes:

WORDS ARE TOOLS OF WRITER'S TRADE—REMBRANDT

"We are going to use the *Editorial board concept*—judging progress of everyone's stories including my comments along the way . . . because it is going to expose you to what you can expect . . . from a magazine editor or *BOARD OF DIRECTORS* . . . you will begin to develop the tough skin you will need in the writing game . . . difficult but not impossible . . ." He discussed story length quality, quantity, balance, feel. He told students to draw ideas from their own experiences. He emphasized a *framework* which he described as *entertaining, informative, series, humorous, or satirical.*

The Reynolds School announced Laxalt's spring semester class with a special poster:

From Journalism to Literature

Seminar by

Robert Laxalt

Author of *Sweet Promised Land* and *A Man in the Wheatfield*

Former UP correspondent

Director Emeritus of the University of Nevada Press

Distinguished Visiting Professor, UNR Department of Journalism

A study of the works of authors who bridged the gap from news writing to novels and short stories

Stephen Crane – Jack London – John Steinbeck – Ernest Hemingway – Frederick Forsyth – and a review of two books by Robert Laxalt.

Aimed at developing students' writing styles, use of plot, settings, characters, personal experiences.

The enrollment would be limited to eight to ten students who were to be selected based on a two-page paper addressing the question: Why I want to take this course.

Laxalt emphasized human character and writer detachment as students analyzed Hemingway's *The Old Man and the Sea,* Steinbeck's *The Red Pony,* Stephen Crane's *The Red Badge of Courage,* the works of Jack London, and other authors. He challenged students: Why do writers write? He provided answers: To say something. To be read. To share an experience with others. Money. Fame. Satisfaction of ego. That is real and worthwhile, too. TO KNOW MORE ABOUT ONE'S SELF. Creative urge. Therapy. Compulsion. To inform.

Laxalt shared ideas he had learned thirty-three years earlier from acclaimed author Walter Van Tilburg Clark. As a United Press reporter, Laxalt had yearned to develop himself as a better writer. He turned to Clark, author of *The City of Trembling Leaves, The Ox-Bow Incident,* and *The Track of the*

Cat. He did not have far to go because the author, celebrated for his work from New York publishing to Hollywood films, was living in an old mansion in Virginia City.[14]

In a conversation at Clark's favorite saloon, the nearby Sazarac on the main street of Virginia City, the author wrote out on a piece of paper a list of what he called *serious* books that he thought *serious* writers should read: Joseph Conrad's *Heart of Darkness,* D. H. Lawrence's *Sons and Lovers,* Dostoevsky's *Crime and Punishment,* Faulkner's *The Sound and the Fury,* Stephen Crane's *The Red Badge of Courage*—and twenty-four more.

Laxalt folded the piece of paper and put in in his shirt pocket. He kept the list for decades and eventually created his own list that he passed on to his students with the same message. Writers must read serious books if they are serious about writing.

Laxalt's list included Jack London's *The Call of the Wild,* John Steinbeck's *Of Mice and Men* and *The Grapes of Wrath*, Tolstoy's *War and Peace*, Mark Twain's *Tom Sawyer* and *Huck Finn,* Hemingway's *The Old Man and the Sea.* Laxalt added Hugo's *Les Misérables*, F. Scott Fitzgerald's *The Great Gatsby,* George Orwell's *Animal Farm,* and twenty-two more.

Laxalt's teaching drew the attention of professional writers as well as students. Charles Kuralt, creator of CBS News's "On the Road" features and anchor of the network's Sunday morning show, read many of Laxalt's books and addressed students during a visit to the Reno campus.[15]

"If you want to be a fine writer, do not emulate me on television, but go to the mountain. When you reach the top of the mountain, Robert Laxalt will be there for you," Kuralt said.

Laxalt continued to teach in his eighteenth year at the journalism school. But his health was failing at age seventy-seven. He suffered a chronic cough and shortness of breath that required a special nebulizer machine to deliver bronchodilator medications to his lungs.[16] This caused him to leave the classroom and meet with students at home. He and his wife, Joyce, a playwright in college and creative partner throughout his career, welcomed students to their home in a pine forest a few miles north of Carson City in Washoe Valley.

Laxalt continued working on another book as his health failed. He was admitted to Saint Mary's Hospital in Reno, treated for lower gastrointestinal bleeding, when he died March 23, 2001, at age seventy-seven. The news moved over the wires of The Associated Press from his boyhood hometown, Carson City, to New York, from Boise to Bilbao, and to the far corners of the globe where his writing was revered.

More than five hundred people filled the University of Nevada, Reno's Nightingale Hall to mourn his death and celebrate his life. his daughters Monique and Kristin read from *Sweet Promised Land.* His son, Bruce, offered a eulogy: "He was born an immigrant kid . . . He grew up tough and scrappy in Carson . . ." bonding with his brothers " . . . who grew close in a wordless way . . . and that time—that season—shaped him forever. . . . And now is the time and the season," his son continued, "for Robert Laxalt—the writer—to live and breathe forever in the limes and pages of his work . . . and in the souls of his readers . . . and through the written voices of his students . . . and *thei*r students as they take the proud duty of passing the torch and continue the lonely work of slowly honing their craft."

Few at the memorial other than immediate family and closest friends were aware that Laxalt has been working on another manuscript. *Travels with My Royal, A Memoir of the Writing Life* was published by the University of Nevada Press within months of his death. The book was a combination of his journalistic and his literary quests. He reported on his early work in chapters titled "My Writing Life Begins," "Reporting Days," and "My First Gangster." He then wrote about a "Transition" toward literature with titles such as "Genesis of

Sweet Promised Land," "A Man in the Wheatfield," and "A Cup of Tea in Pamplona." He added a postscript examining "The Writing Life."

To honor his legacy and inspire new generations, the Reynolds School of Journalism created the Robert Laxalt Distinguished Writer Program in 2004 to share experience with students and the public. The first honoree was *National Geographic* photojournalist William Albert Allard, who had worked with Laxalt on the book *A Time We Knew, Images of Yesterday in the Basque Homeland.*[17] Others who have followed include national humanities scholar and author Clay Jenkinson, novelist James Houston, investigative reporter and Pulitzer Prize winner Isabel Wilkerson of *The New York Times*, investigative book journalist Sally Denton, and, in 2022, Beth Piatote, an Indigenous language activist, playwright, creative writer, and scholar.

Laxalt's life as a writer poses questions: was he forever the reporter of his youthful days or was there an illusive mixture and perhaps even a smooth blend as he rose to literary heights? For readers who know him only through his literature, the challenge now is to determine how and why he came to be the unique storyteller that he was. In the opinion of this longtime friend and colleague, Robert Laxalt did what Hemingway, Steinbeck, Jack London, and other journalists-turned-authors did. He searched for the best way to tell each story, and he achieved it.

Notes

1 Robert Laxalt, Citations from newspaper stories in Laxalt papers, 85–09, Box 13, Special Collections and Archives, University of Nevada Reno Libraries.

2 Laxalt, "The Library and I" (Reno: Black Rock Press University of Nevada, 1999).

3 Laxalt papers, 85–09, Box 13.

4 Warren Lerude, Robert Laxalt, *The Story of a Storyteller* (Reno: Center for Basque Studies Press, 2013), 58–60. Author interview with Joyce Laxalt, April 2010.

5 Laxalt papers, 85–09, Box 13.

6 Laxalt papers, 85–09, Box 25.

7 Laxalt papers, 85–09, Box 9.

8 Lerude, Robert Laxalt, *The Story of a Storyteller*, 87.

9 Ibid 94–95; Robert Laxalt, *The Violent Land* (Reno: Nevada Publishing Company, 1953) 1–7.

10 Laxalt papers, 85–09, Box 1; Robert Laxalt, *Travels with My Royal* (Reno: University of Nevada Press, 2001) 140. Lerude, Roberti Laxalt, *The Story of a Storyteller*, 127. Author interview with Joyce Laxalt, October 2009).

11 Robert Laxalt, *Sweet Promised Land* 50th Anniversary Edition (Reno: University of Nevada Press, 2007), Review page note.

12 Robert Laxalt, *A Man in the Wheatfield* (New York: Harper & Row, 1964) Cover Statement, Laxalt papers, 85–09, press clippings.

13 Laxalt, papers, 85–09, Box 23.

14 Walter Van Tilburg Clark, *The City of Trembling Leaves* (New York: Random House, 1945), reprinted by University of Nevada Press, 1991, Foreword by Robert Laxalt), xiii.

15 Lerude, Robert Laxalt, *The Story of a Storyteller*, 228. Author recollection, Scripps Howard dinner, University of Nevada, Reno, April, 1984

16 Lerude, Robert Laxalt, *The Story of a Storyteller*, 225. Correspondence with Dr. Kristin Laxalt, August, 2011.

17 William Albert Allard, Robert Laxalt, *A Time We Knew* (Reno: University of Nevada Press, 1990).

Robert Laxalt's Basqueness through Sweet Promised Land

An Introduction

by Xabier Irujo

"My father was a sheepherder, and his home was the hills" is the opening sentence of *Sweet Promised Land* by Robert Laxalt and sets the tone for the entire memoir.[1] The land, the hills, and the sheep are all important aspects of Basque identity, culture, and way of life. Overall, the sentence serves to introduce the central themes of the book: family, identity, connection to the land, and the importance of tradition and heritage.

The book provides a rich and nuanced portrait of Basque culture and history, and it offers readers a powerful glimpse into the complexities of identity, heritage, and belonging. Through Laxalt's writing, readers are able to discover his Basqueness and gain a deeper appreciation for the diverse and vibrant culture of the Basques. *Sweet Promised Land* is a powerful exploration of the author's Basque identity and heritage, and it offers readers a vivid and deeply personal glimpse into the complex history and culture of the Basque people. Laxalt delves into the challenges faced by Basque immigrants in the US, including discrimination and marginalization, and the ways in which they have preserved and celebrated their cultural traditions despite these obstacles. Throughout the book, Laxalt weaves together personal anecdotes and family history with broader cultural and historical themes, creating a rich and nuanced portrait of Basque culture and the immigrant experience. By exploring the complexities of identity and belonging through the lens of his own experiences and heritage, the author invites readers to reflect on their own sense of identity and the forces that shape it.

The memoir is initially set in Nevada, where Laxalt's family settled after emigrating from the Northern Basque Country. Laxalt's father, Dominique, was a sheepherder who spent long months away from home tending to his flock. Laxalt and his siblings were raised by their mother, who worked tirelessly to provide for her family. In Robert's words, they were born in a little house, in a little town, in a little valley surrounded by great mountains; as children they walked across the hills, and down into the valleys, and through the woods, and along the rivers. They walked until their feet were sore and their legs were tired, but their spirits were high and their hearts were full. They were surrounded by the sound of bells, the smell of cheese, the taste of cider, the touch of wool. There was a peace in that valley, a stillness in that air, a sense of timelessness that was almost palpable.

The book chronicles Laxalt's childhood, his relationships with his family and friends, and his experiences growing up in a rural, isolated community. Laxalt describes the hardships and challenges his family faced, including poverty, prejudice, and the harsh realities of life in the American West. Laxalt describes how his mother was a key figure in the family's immigration journey, providing support and encouragement to her husband, Dominique, as they faced the challenges of adapting to a new culture and building a life in America. She is also depicted as a hardworking and resourceful woman who was able to adapt to the demands of life in the American West.

Laxalt's mother is also shown to be a source of cultural continuity for the family, helping to pass on Basque traditions and values to her children. She is depicted as a skilled cook, who prepares traditional Basque dishes for her family and friends, and as a devoted mother who instills in her children a deep sense of pride in their cultural heritage. Laxalt embodies and reflects the defining traits of the Basque people who have settled in the United States. The Basques, renowned for their pride, are a fiercely independent community, deeply rooted in their ancestral lands. They possess a language unlike any other, a testament to their distinct cultural identity. Their rich and ancient heritage is characterized by vibrant traditions, folklore, and culinary delights that have stood the test of time. The Basque way of life, with its strong sense of community and respect for tradition, has endured for centuries, forging a resilient and enduring bond between the Basque diaspora and their cherished homeland.[2]

Dominique decides to take Robert with him on a trip to the Basque Country to visit their relatives and see the land of their ancestors because, rephrasing George Santayana, "a man who forgets his past is a man who is lost in the present."[3] Both of Dominique's parents have passed away by the time he returns to the Basque Country. His mother died when he was still a young man and his father passed away later in life, after Dominique had already left to pursue his fortunes in America.[4] The trip is an important moment of connection for father and son, as they bond over their shared heritage and the experiences of their journey.

Dominique seeks to reconnect with his family roots and visit the land of his elders. He wants to show his son the place where he grew up and introduce him to his relatives who still live there. He also spends time with his childhood friends, some of whom have become successful businessmen and businesswomen in the region. Dominique feels a strong connection to his Basque heritage, and he wants to share that connection with his son.

During their trip, they visit the village where Dominique was born, meet his relatives, and learn more about their family history. Robert's mother, Theresa Alpetche, was born in 1891 in Baigorri, the town of the red river in the Northern Basque Country.[5] The Laxalt family's ancestral town is Atharratze, also in the Northern Basque Country. It was there, under the shadow of the Pyrenees, that his father's ancestors had lived for centuries. It is where the Laxalts were born and raised before immigrating to the United States in the early 1900s. Robert describes his family's connection to the town and its surrounding countryside, noting the importance of the region's rugged beauty and rich cultural heritage in shaping his family's identity and values. There was something about Atharratze that felt like home to him, even though he had never been there before.

Despite living thousands of miles away from their ancestral home, they maintain a deep sense of connection to their roots, and this connection is a central theme of the book. The trip provides an opportunity for Dominique to reconnect with his past and to reflect on his life in America as a Basque immigrant. During their trip, Dominique and Robert visit many other places in the Basque Country, including Pamplona. They also spend time in the rural areas of the country, including the mountainous areas where Basque shepherds tend their flocks. As they sit by the trees, they feel that deep sense of connection to their roots. They come to appreciate the deep cultural significance of the tree in Basque culture and the many stories and traditions it represents. They also visit town markets, where they sample local foods and observe the hustle and bustle of daily life and walk along the main street of little villages, passing little shops selling souvenirs and Basque handicrafts. Additionally, they witness a traditional Basque dance performance in the town's square, which further underscores the book's exploration of culture and tradition.

The family house is portrayed as a symbol of the enduring value of family ties and cultural heritage.[6] The house has been passed down through several generations of Dominique's family, and it serves as a physical link to the family's history and traditions. When Dominique returns to the Basque Country, he feels a deep sense of connection to the house and the land it occupies, and he recognizes the importance of preserving this legacy for future generations. The past was gone, but it was not forgotten. It lived on in the stories that were told, in the songs that were sung, in the dances that were danced. Throughout the book, the family house is also depicted as a gathering place for family and community celebrations, such as weddings and religious festivals. These gatherings serve as an important reminder of the power of shared experiences and communal bonds to strengthen and sustain individuals and communities. The family house serves as a powerful symbol of the enduring value of family and cultural heritage in the face of change and uncertainty.

While the family house serves as an important setting in *Sweet Promised Land* and plays a central role in many of the book's key themes and motifs that contribute to its rich and complex tapestry,[7] there are hints that the ownership of the house may be a point of contention among various family members. For example, Dominique's siblings express concern that the house may be sold or lost to the family because of financial difficulties. Additionally, Dominique himself is reluctant to leave the house unoccupied during his extended stay in the United States, suggesting that he may feel a sense of responsibility for its upkeep and preservation.

Robert portrays his family as frequently gathering around the table for meals, both lunch and dinner.[8] These meals are an important part of the family's daily routine, and they often serve as a time for the family to discuss their experiences and share stories. In fact, the meals that the family shares together are often described in detail in the book, with descriptions of the food they eat, the conversations they have, and the rituals and traditions that accompany the meals. For example, the family often serves traditional Basque dishes such as lamb stew and chorizo, and they have specific ways of preparing and serving the food that reflect their cultural heritage.

The meals are usually prepared by the women of the family who are depicted as skilled cooks able to prepare traditional Basque dishes. They are also shown to be very resourceful, using the vegetables and herbs grown in the family's garden to add flavor and nutrition to the meals. They often help each other in the kitchen and are shown to be particularly talented at making desserts and pastries.

The rituals and traditions surrounding the meals they share are a significant part of the book's depiction of family life and culture. For instance, grace before meals is an important ritual among Basques. Before they start eating, the Laxalt family members say a prayer in Basque, thanking God for the food and asking for His blessings. Serving food family-style is another important element that Robert had known since he was very young in Carson City. The food is served in large dishes and passed around the table, with each person taking what they want. This communal style of dining reflects the importance of sharing and generosity in Basque culture. The use of specific dishes and utensils is another important cultural element of the family meals. The family often uses traditional Basque dishes and utensils, such as earthenware bowls and wooden spoons, to serve and eat their food. This reflects the family's connection to their cultural heritage and the importance of tradition in their lives. Lastly, storytelling and conversation are elemental aspects of a Basque meal. The family members often share stories and engage in lively conversation, reflecting the importance of socializing and community: "Enough of memories for now. Let's us have a toast and a *kantu* for the prodigal who has returned!"[9]

Siblings often wake up early in the morning to tend to the family's livestock, and they spend long hours working in the fields or doing other labor. This work can be physically exhausting, and it may leave little time or energy for leisure activities or relaxation. In this regard, the family's mealtimes are depicted as a time of respite and enjoyment, a time to come together and share stories and experiences. The meals and dining times in the book are seen as a source of comfort and support, providing a sense of stability and routine amid the family's demanding and often unpredictable lives.

The author describes the meals shared by the Laxalt family with great detail and warmth, suggesting that they hold a special place in his heart. It seems that Robert viewed the meals shared in *Sweet Promised Land* as a key part of his own Basqueness and a cherished memory of his childhood and family life. The similarities between these meals and those he experienced in his own home suggest that the book draws heavily on Robert's personal experiences and memories characterized by a strong sense of tradition, with an emphasis on sharing, generosity, and community.

However, the house is not necessarily the only or primary background curtain of the book. In addition to the family house, the book explores a range of other settings and landscapes, including the rugged terrain of the Basque Country, the bustling cities of Reno and San Francisco, and the expansive vistas of the American West. Each of these settings contributes to the book's larger themes of cultural identity, migration, and the search for belonging. Furthermore, the book's characters and their relationships also play a critical role in shaping the story and its overarching themes. Through the experiences of Dominique, Robert, and their extended family, the book explores the complexities of family dynamics, the challenges of communication across cultural and generational divides, and the enduring power of love and connection to overcome even the most difficult of circumstances.

The trip to the Basque Country deepens the reader's understanding of Dominique's character and his relationship with his son, as well as providing insight into the cultural heritage of the Basque people. The trip also provides an opportunity for Dominique to reflect on his life in America and his experiences as a Basque immigrant.

Robert describes the natural beauty of the Basque Country, with its rugged mountains, lush green valleys, and picturesque villages. He describes it like a great tapestry, woven of the threads of the past and the present, a living tapestry that changed with the seasons and the years, yet remained unbroken and whole. He is also struck by the rich cultural heritage of the region, with its distinctive language, music, dance, and culinary traditions. Robert is particularly moved by the warmth and hospitality of the Basque people, who welcome him and his father into their homes and share their customs and traditions with them. He is also impressed by the strong sense of community and cooperation that he observes among the Basque people, which he sees as a key to their success as a cultural group. As Robert puts it, they were bound for the Basque Country, a land of rolling hills and jagged peaks, of ancient stone farmhouses and clanging church bells, where the language was like no other, and the people lived close to the land, as they had for centuries. A land where everything looked like it had been there for a thousand years.[10]

Robert makes a conscious effort to familiarize himself with basic Basque phrases and fully immerse himself in the local culture. Throughout the book, he shares various Basque expressions with the reader, "like an Eskualduna."[11] He is also deeply moved by the music, dance, and other cultural expressions of the Basque people, which suggest a deep connection to his ancestral roots. He spends time with his aunt Marie and her family. He also spends time with his cousins, who coach him about the history and culture of the Basque Country. However, Robert expresses a sense of being a stranger in his own land, as he grapples with the complex and often contradictory aspects of his identity as a Basque American. On the one hand, he feels deeply connected to his Basque cultural heritage and takes great pride in his ancestry. He admires the resilience, hard work, and strong family ties of the Basque people, and he is moved by their warmth and hospitality. Laxalt acknowledges the profound bond between the Basque people and their land, as well as their strong interconnectedness, which he views as a source of strength and beauty. He observed that this connection provided them with resilience during challenging times and remained instrumental in shaping their lives and culture up to his time.

On the other hand, Robert also feels a sense of disconnection and alienation from his Basque heritage, as he struggles to reconcile his American upbringing with his ancestral roots. He grapples with the tension between his desire to embrace his Basque identity and his sense of being an outsider in both American and Basque contexts. From his standpoint, the Basque land is like a proud and aging woman, whose beauty still lingers on, but whose strength is fading.

One of the key factors contributing to Robert's sense of estrangement from Basque culture is the language barrier. Although Robert has a basic knowledge of the Basque language, he does not speak it fluently, which can create feelings of disconnection and isolation. Another factor is the complexity of Basque cultural traditions and customs, which can be difficult for outsiders to fully understand and appreciate. For example, Robert is initially puzzled by the Basque tradition of herding, which plays a central role in

Basque culture and identity, but which he initially perceives as archaic and impractical.

His sense of feeling estranged by the Basque culture reflects the challenges of navigating a complex and multifaceted cultural identity, and the difficulty of reconciling different aspects of one's personal history and heritage. Robert's sense of being a stranger in his own land reflects the complex and often fraught experience of immigrant communities, who must navigate the challenges of preserving their cultural heritage while also adapting to new cultural contexts and forging their own path in the world.

Robert Laxalt observes the complicated dynamics of Dominique's relationship with his siblings, and how these dynamics have shaped Dominique's personality and outlook on life. The son recognizes the deep bond of love and loyalty that exists between Dominique and his siblings, despite their occasional conflicts and disagreements, and he notes that the years that passed during his absence from the old country held no significance or had no impact.[12] He admires the way that his uncles and aunts and other siblings support and care for each other, even in difficult times, and sees this as a reflection of the strong family values that are central to Basque culture. At the same time, however, Robert also perceives a certain tension and distance in Dominique's relationship with his siblings, particularly his brother Maurice. He notes that Dominique often seems to feel overshadowed or inferior to Maurice, who is more successful in business and more outgoing and gregarious in social situations. This dynamic, Robert suggests, has contributed to Dominique's tendency to be more reserved and introspective, and to value the quieter, more contemplative aspects of life.

Robert is also captivated by his aunt Marie-Jeanne, Dominique's sister, whom he describes as wild and unpredictable and also fiercely independent and self-reliant. Robert admires Marie-Jeanne's resilience and courage in the face of personal challenges and setbacks, and he sees her as a reflection of the strength and resilience that are characteristic of the Basque women. She is not necessarily the archetypical model of Basque women, as the Basque Country and its people are diverse and complex, with a range of personalities and perspectives. However, Marie-Jeanne does embody certain qualities that are often associated with Basque women, such as resilience, independence, and self-reliance. Throughout the book, she is portrayed as a woman who has faced significant challenges in her life, including loss. Despite these difficulties, she remains determined and resourceful, working hard to make a living and provide for her family. At the same time, Marie-Jeanne is also fiercely independent, rejecting traditional gender roles and expectations in favor of carving out her own path in life. She is unafraid to speak her mind and challenge authority, even when doing so puts her at risk of social disapproval.

Another person who captures Robert's attention is Papa Pierre, Dominique's brother-in-law, who embodies the more cosmopolitan and sophisticated side of Basque culture in Montori. Montori is not a sprawling metropolis or a village perched high up in the mountains; rather, it is a small town nestled in the foothills. Its inhabitants do not primarily engage in sheepherding activities, as one might expect in a rural mountainous region. Instead, they comprise a predominantly urban population whose livelihoods are not directly connected to the hills and pastures. Robert is struck by Pierre's elegant manners and refined tastes and sees him as a reminder of the wider world of art and culture that exists beyond the narrow confines of his own upbringing. Robert's relationship with Pierre is only briefly described, but it is complex and multifaceted, reflecting both the similarities and differences that can exist between members of the same family and culture. While the two men may not always see eye to eye, they share a deep respect for their shared heritage and the values that have shaped their lives. Robert begins to develop a deeper appreciation for Pierre, seeing him as a kind of counterpoint to the more rough-and-tumble aspects of Basque culture with which he has grown up. At the same time, however, Robert is also somewhat critical of Pierre's perceived lack of connection to his Basque roots, seeing him as something of an outsider or "other" within the community.

However, Robert is particularly drawn to his elders, who represent an earlier generation of Basque immigrants and a simpler, more traditional way of life. He admires their strength and resilience in the face of adversity, and the way that they embody the values of hard work, honesty, and loyalty that are central to Basque culture. He also appreciates their wisdom and insight, and the way that they offer a different perspective on life than the more materialistic and achievement-oriented outlook of his father and some of his uncles. Through his interactions with the oldest siblings and neighbors, he gains a deeper appreciation for the history and traditions of his Basque heritage, and a sense of connection to a simpler, more authentic way of life. This connection is contrasted with the fast-paced, materialistic world of America that Dominique and some of his other relatives have embraced and highlights the tension between modernity and tradition that runs throughout the book. And yet, despite the changes that had come to the land and its people, he feels that there remained something pure and unbroken, something that spoke of a culture and a way of life that had survived for generations.

As for his father, one of Dominique's main discoveries is a sense of connection to his past and his cultural heritage after forty-seven years of absence "and ten thousand thoughts of home."[13] As he visits the village where he was born and meets his relatives, he is reminded of the customs and traditions with which he grew up. This experience helps him to understand his own identity as a Basque immigrant in America and to feel a deeper sense of pride in his cultural heritage. Dominique is especially connected to his sister Marie and her family. Marie is portrayed as a strong and caring figure who has always been a stabilizing presence in Dominique's life, providing him with love and support even in the face of difficult circumstances. Throughout the book, Dominique's connection to his sister and her family serves as a kind of touchstone for him, a reminder of the love and stability that he has always craved and valued.

In his work, the past is like a river, always flowing, always changing, but never forgotten. When talking to his sister Marie, Dominique confesses in his own way to her that he feels like a traitor leaving them all behind. But he had to go. There was nothing for him here, and he wanted a better life for his family. By leaving for America, he feels that he has abandoned them and betrayed their trust. Moreover, Dominique's sense of guilt is also related to the challenges and sacrifices that he had to make to build a new life in America. As an immigrant, he faced discrimination, isolation, and economic hardship, all of which took a toll on his health, well-being, and family life. This statement reflects Dominique's conflicting emotions—on the one hand, his desire to provide for his family and build a better future, and on the other hand, his sense of responsibility and loyalty to his family and community in the Basque Country.

The book doesn't provide a direct account of how his brothers and sisters see their brother's departure to America. However, we can infer from the portrayal of them and other family members that they were deeply affected by his brother's decision to leave. Marie, like many other Basque women of her time, was raised with a strong sense of family loyalty and duty. She may have felt hurt and betrayed by his departure, which would have left her feeling abandoned and vulnerable. Throughout the book, there are several instances where Dominique expresses his ambivalence about his decision to emigrate, and his sense of loss for the family and community that he left behind.

The book doesn't directly address Robert's feelings about Dominique's return, as many years had already passed by the time he returned to the Basque Country. Like many parents, he likely wanted his children to be happy and fulfilled, even if this meant making difficult choices and sacrifices along the way. Ultimately, the book suggests that Dominique's departure to America was a difficult and painful decision, one that had profound consequences for both him and his family

Another important discovery for Dominique is the realization that he has achieved a level of success and prosperity in America that he never would have been able to attain in the Basque Country. This realization gives him a new sense of appreciation for the opportunities that America has provided him and his family. Despite these feelings of guilt and regret, however, Dominique ultimately finds a way to reconcile his past and present, drawing strength and inspiration from both his Basque heritage and his American experiences. By the end of the book, he is able to embrace both sides of his identity, recognizing the value of his roots while also celebrating the opportunities and freedoms that America has afforded him and his family.

Finally, Dominique's trip to the Basque Country strengthens his bond with his son.

Dominique is proud of Robert's accomplishments and admires his intelligence, curiosity, and deep sense of respect for his cultural heritage. Dominique also sees Robert as a source of continuity for the family, who will carry on their traditions and values into the future. Dominique's family sees Robert as a respectful and thoughtful young man. They admire his intelligence, his work ethic, and his willingness to learn from his elders and engage with Basque traditions and customs. Mostly, they respect the young son's love and reverence for his father. They also see him as a source of hope and pride for the family, who will carry on their legacy and pass on their traditions to future generations. Dominique and his family see Robert as a key figure in their family's story, who embodies their cultural values and represents the promise of their collective future. They are proud of him and supportive of his journey of self-discovery, which they see as an essential part of his growth and development as a person.

Through their shared experiences and conversations during the trip, Dominique is able to pass on his love for his cultural heritage to his son and deepen their relationship. Robert learns that the challenges, downfalls, and triumphs of his father had been challenged only in virtue of the enduring importance of family and cultural heritage. In exchange, family members have lived through a complex process of shaping identity and relationships.

Robert admires his father's ability to adapt to the challenges of life in America and his commitment to providing for his family and preserving their cultural traditions: "He was the adventurer who had braved the unknown land across the sea and found his fortune."[14]. Robert also comes to appreciate the importance of being a father and acting as such, as he observes his own father's close relationship with his family members and his desire to pass on his cultural heritage to his son. Through their travels to the Basque Country, Robert sees firsthand the significance of family and cultural traditions in his father's life, and how they have shaped his identity and success. That pride resulted in a key element for his own success in life.

During the trip, Dominique gains a deeper understanding of himself and his cultural heritage. He reflects on the values and traditions that have shaped his life and his family's experiences as immigrants in America. Through his conversations with his son and his relatives in the Basque Country, he is able to process his thoughts and feelings and gain new insights into his own life: "Out of the past the memories have come, born in an old album with faded pictures of another time and another way of life in a land thousands of miles away."[15]

The trip also allows Dominique to gain a new perspective on his own success and achievements in America. By visiting the impoverished villages of the Basque Country, he is able to appreciate the opportunities and privileges that he and his family have enjoyed in America. Laxalt vividly describes the customs and traditions of the Basque people, and how those customs were preserved and adapted in the American West. He also depicts the difficulties that his family and other Basque immigrants faced in adjusting to a new culture and language, as well as the discrimination they often encountered.

Dominique's trip to the Basque Country is a powerful and introspective journey that helps him to better understand himself and his place in the world. It allows him to reconnect with his past, his culture, and his family roots, which helps him to gain new insights into his own life and experiences. So he thinks, in life, we are all travelers on a journey, seeking our place in the world.

Love is like a river that flows through life, sometimes calm, sometimes rough, but always there. Despite all the difficulties in life, *Sweet Promised Land* is ultimately a celebration of his family's resilience and their love for one another. The book offers a poignant and deeply personal portrait of a family and a community that have been largely overlooked in the broader history of the American prairies: "And suddenly before me, I saw the West rising up at dawn with an awesome vastness of deserts and mighty mountain ranges."[16]

Sweet Promised Land is a beautifully written and heartfelt memoir that offers a unique perspective on the immigrant experience in the American West. It is a rich and evocative portrait of a cultural community and the immigrant experience that provides insight into the challenges and triumphs of Basque immigrants in America, and the enduring importance of family and cultural heritage in shaping identity and relationships.

The attachment to family values and cooperativism is portrayed as one of the most precious values of Basque culture and a key to success according to Robert Laxalt in *Sweet Promised Land*. Throughout the book, Laxalt describes how the Basque people have a strong sense of family loyalty and community cooperation, which are integral to their cultural identity. These values are seen as essential to the success of Basque immigrants in America, helping them to adapt to a new environment and build a sense of community and support.

When Dominique and Robert return to Nevada from their trip to the Basque Country, they are described as being "different people." They bring with them a deepened appreciation for the importance of family, community, and tradition. Throughout their journey, Dominique and Robert witness firsthand the power of strong family ties and community support in Basque culture, which enables individuals to weather difficult times and find meaning and purpose in their lives. They also learn about the importance of preserving cultural traditions and passing them down to future generations, as a way of honoring the past and connecting with one's roots. Perhaps most importantly, Dominique and Robert return from their trip with a renewed sense of connection to each other, as father and son. Through their shared experiences and conversations, they are able to bridge the gaps that had previously divided them, and to deepen their understanding and appreciation of each other as individuals.

Throughout *Sweet Promised Land*, Robert and Dominique Laxalt emphasize the importance of love and relationships in achieving personal fulfillment and success in life. They recognize that material success and achievements are only possible through a strong family connection; moreover, after their trip father and son acknowledge that material conquests are ultimately empty and unsatisfying without deeper connections to other people. Dominique reflects on the loneliness and isolation he experienced as a young man pursuing his dreams of success, and the way that his eventual marriage and family gave him a deeper sense of purpose and meaning. Love and relationships are seen as integral to this process, providing a sense of meaning and fulfillment in life.

As Robert Laxalt wrote, in the end, it is the love and the connection that we share with others that gives our lives meaning and purpose. It is the love of family and friends, the love of our homeland and our heritage, that makes life sweet and promises to endure beyond our time on this earth.

Notes

1 Laxalt, Robert, *Sweet Promised Land*, University of Nevada Press, Reno & Las Vegas, 2007, 1.

2 *Congressional Record: Proceedings and Debates of the 91st Congress. First Session*, United States Printing Office, Washington DC, vol. 115, part 17, 22935–22936.

3 In his four-part investigation titled *The Life of Reason*, specifically in volume one *Reason in Common Sense*, published in 1905–06, George Santayana, a philosophy professor at Harvard University, conveyed the idea that progress does not come from mere change; it relies on the ability to retain. If change becomes absolute, there is no foundation for improvement, and no path is established for potential progress. Similarly, if experiences are not remembered, as is the case among primitive societies, they are doomed to forever remain in a state of infancy. Santayana famously declared that "those who cannot remember the past are condemned to repeat it."

4 Laxalt, Robert, *Sweet Promised Land*, University of Nevada Press, Reno & Las Vegas, 2007, 111.

5 Baigorri literally translates from Basque "Ibai" (meaning river) and "gorri" (meaning red.).

6 Laxalt, Robert, *Sweet Promised Land*, University of Nevada Press, Reno & Las Vegas, 1986, 131.

7 Laxalt, Robert, *Sweet Promised Land*, University of Nevada Press, Reno & Las Vegas, 1986, 120.

8 Laxalt, Robert, *Sweet Promised Land*, University of Nevada Press, Reno & Las Vegas, 1986, 175.

9 Laxalt, Robert, *Sweet Promised Land*, University of Nevada Press, Reno & Las Vegas, 2007, 115.

10 Laxalt, Robert, *Sweet Promised Land*, University of Nevada Press, Reno & Las Vegas, 2007, 115.

11 "Like a Basque speaker." Laxalt, Robert, *Sweet Promised Land*, University of Nevada Press, Reno & Las Vegas, 2007, 38.

12 Laxalt, Robert, *Sweet Promised Land*, University of Nevada Press, Reno & Las Vegas, 2007, 115.

13 Laxalt, Robert, *Sweet Promised Land*, University of Nevada Press, Reno & Las Vegas, 2007, 94.

14 Laxalt, Robert, *Sweet Promised Land*, University of Nevada Press, Reno & Las Vegas, 2007, 110.

15 Laxalt, Robert, *Sweet Promised Land*, University of Nevada Press, Reno & Las Vegas, 1986, 147.

16 Laxalt, Robert, *Sweet Promised Land*, University of Nevada Press, Reno & Las Vegas, 1986, 158.

In Search of Sweet Promised Land

Teaching a Basque American Memoir

by Sandra Ott and Mariann Vaczi

Robert Laxalt's wonderful memoir, *Sweet Promised Land*, offers a very personal lens through which to understand a father-son relationship in one of Nevada's most well-known Basque families; it also has relevance, both deep and broad, to a range of ever important issues: the experience of migrants, the physical, economic, social, and emotional challenges they face during their journeys from the homeland to new and usually unknown destinations; return migration and cultural dissonance; and, among others, intergenerational and cultural misunderstandings, and how these are overcome or exacerbated. *Sweet Promised Land* entails much more than the physical journey of Dominique Laxalt and his son Robert to Dominique's natal province in the French Basque Country.

As coauthors of this chapter, we provide a unique perspective on Laxalt's best-known and widely praised work through the voices of our students at the University of Nevada, Reno, and through our academic training as cultural anthropologists who have done extensive fieldwork in the Basque Country and teach courses on Basque Culture. On average, about forty undergraduates enroll in the online version of that course, which is offered once a year and taught by Mariann Vaczi. An additional twenty-five to thirty students take Sandra Ott's Basque Culture class in person every fall. Both versions include a module on *Sweet Promised Land*. Our students typically major in a wide range of disciplines, but many study anthropology. Normally only a few are of Basque descent in any one semester, so teaching the memoir provides a unique opportunity not just to reflect about immigration, but also to spread cultural knowledge about the Basque diaspora to Nevada's youth. How do they and other American undergraduates respond to this memoir? What relevance does it have for their lives? Our chapter charts the responses of several generations of UNR students to such questions. Because of the very different nature of these classes, we teach Laxalt's work in quite different ways.

Students who study the memoir online communicate with one another and professor Vaczi through chat lines and discussion threads. By contrast, students who take Basque Culture in person can form a different kind of intellectual community through small group discussions, face-to-face dialogue with their instructor, and guest speakers from the Basque American community. They are also able to access material culture relating to Dominique Laxalt's sheep camp and to Theresa Laxalt's private papers, thanks to the Laxalt collection held at the Jon Bilbao Library, which shares premises with UNR's Center for Basque Studies. In addition, students use photographic collections that feature the small Basque town of Tardets (Atharratze) and the nearby farmhouse in which Dominique grew up in the Northern Basque province of Zuberoa (Xiberoa in the local dialect, Soule in French) in the early decades of the twentieth century.[1] Ott has conducted fieldwork in that area for forty-seven years and thus brings personal experience of rural Basque culture, Laxalt's natal community, and its citizens to the classroom.

The in-person course is divided into three modules: the first focuses on Basques in the northern provinces, in southwestern France; the second on Basques in the southern provinces, in Spain; and the third module examines Basques in the American West. All three modules explore the range of ways in which urban and rural Basque identity is shaped: traditionally by the rural Basque house, the local form of Catholicism, the "first neighbor" relationship, and Basque customary laws that long served as a kind of bill of rights for Basques in the seven historic territories. In more modern times, and especially in the southern Basque Country, other institutionalized relationships and practices play a major role in defining the individual: ranging from lifelong friendship groups (*cuadrillas*) and associated street-based rituals of barhopping to gastronomic societies and soccer fandom (especially in Bilbao). In the third module, students learn about identity formation in the American West, migration from the Basque Country, and the challenges Basques faced because of their perceived ethnic difference, language, and socioeconomic status. Students explore the important roles played by Basque women in their new homeland and their relationships with husbands, brothers, and other family members who became involved in sheepherding and in running Basque boarding houses and hotels. The last three classes of the course focus on *Sweet Promised Land*, a text that enables students to reconnect with the course's first module about traditional rural French Basque culture. The knowledge they gained at the start of the course gives them a firm base upon which to evaluate Dominique's (and to a lesser extent) his wife's experiences as immigrants in Nevada and the culture from which they came.

In the first of three classes devoted to the memoir, students contemplate Dominique's character through multiple lenses: life in the sheep camp, its hardships and dangers (mountain lions, among others), and its impact upon his wife, Theresa, and their children. Students are encouraged to think about gender roles in the context of the 1950s and 1960s "old Reno" and northern Nevada culture at that time. They are struck by Theresa, her independence, stubbornness, and her physical and emotional strength. Students connect such traits in both Theresa and Dominique to rural Basque values: the Basques' hard work ethic, the importance of physical and spiritual strength (*indarra*, a Basque concept that students always find fascinating), the rural Basque house as a source of social and spiritual identity, and the key role played by the female head of household in raising the children and keeping the house "in order." Students also relate Theresa's independence to the experiences of rural French Basque women during the First World War, when women often ran both household and farm in the absence (and all too often the death) of their menfolk.[2]

The memoir's famous opening lines are not lost upon students in their efforts to relate Laxalt's memoir to rural Basque values: "My father was a sheepherder, and his home was the hills." The Laxalt home in Carson City did not define Dominique's identity; the Sierra, his flocks, and shepherding way of life did. Students seek to understand Dominique's character, choices, and actions within the dual cultural context of his lifetime: the rural Basque countryside he left behind and the rugged terrain and equally rugged men (and women) of the Sierra Nevada that became the fabric of Dominique's daily life in the American West. Students reflect upon the extent to which a person bears the imprint of a former way of life in the homeland in their new socio-cultural surroundings as an immigrant. Dominique came from upper Zuberoa, where daily life revolved around the livestock and agriculture that supported its small farms and trips to the market town of Tardets, a small, densely nucleated hub of socializing and commerce. By 1976, when Ott first did fieldwork in upper Zuberoa, traditional rural Basque values and social institutions remained intact: cooperation, mutual aid, and trust characterized relations within the household and between "first neighbors." Everyone in the household was expected to work for the common good of the house, not for their own individual goals. To what extent did Dominique retain those values and expectations as a sheepherder in Nevada? Students' discussions often conclude that he did not always behave in a manner that reflected his cultural roots in rural Zuberoa. His long absences and occasional disappearances in the Sierra caused considerable angst among his family members. As a student once observed in an essay, Dominique regularly caused the *indarra* of his house to be "in disarray," an observation linked to Ott's ethnographic study of a Xiberoan shepherding community and the importance of keeping a household free of conflict and disorder.[3]

Students who are themselves immigrants or the children and grandchildren of immigrants always bring fresh perspectives to Dominique's experiences when they talk about the cultures of their family's origins and the challenges they faced on coming to the United States. *Sweet Promised Land* has great relevance for our own times.

The memoir also generates discussion in class about intergenerational relationships and differing attitudes held by parents and children toward material possessions, toward change, and racial and ethnic otherness. Students often relate Dominique's reluctance to surrender his wedding suit to similar behavior displayed by their own grandparents. The discussion readily turns to an evaluation of contemporary acquisitive practices in American society. Does one really need more material possessions? On a deeper level, students examine intergenerational misunderstandings between Robert and his father; the ways in which each individual handled and perceived Dominique's standoff with the mountain lion; their encounters with Puerto Ricans in the airport as they prepared for departure to France; and their sojourn back to Zuberoa, after Dominique's absence of forty-seven years.

The last class of the course concentrates on the very different experiences of Dominique and Robert on their return to Tardets; their reunions with Dominique's sisters and other kin; and encounters with local people, young and old. The final section of the memoir leads students to talk about the meaning of "home" in their own lives: home as a physical space, as a "sensation" or feeling, and as an idea that might sometimes entail multiple physical spaces.[4] Students with family roots outside the United States often reflect poignantly on the multidimensional meaning of a return "home," how different generations in a family perceive such a journey, and the process of discovering where one truly belongs.

Students of Basque descent who have had the opportunity to visit the Basque Country and/or who know something about their family background are rare in the Basque Culture class, but they always add to student engagement with *Sweet Promised Land*. This is particularly striking when they talk about the experiences of their own grandparents or great-grandparents as immigrants in the American West. Some twenty years ago, when Ott taught Basque Culture, a student brought her Basque grandparents to class. They shyly spoke about early experiences in northern Nevada as immigrants, how they met in Susanville, California, their difficulties with English, and huge cultural changes. Their granddaughter in turn reflected on ways in which the course had shaped her own perceptions not only of the hardships they had endured, but also of the life they forged in Sparks, Nevada. She related some of their daily practices to traditional rural Basque customs (such as making the sign of the cross on a baguette before cutting off the first piece and keeping holy water on the landing of their house so that people could bless themselves while going up and down the stairs). The student and Ott went on to give a joint talk in a local library about her grandparents' journey to and life in Nevada. They sat in the front row and beamed at their granddaughter, content to have her tell their story.

In those early years of teaching Basque Culture, the most beloved guest speakers came to class when students were reading *Sweet Promised Land*: the late Louis Erreguible and his late wife, Lorraine, the founding owners of Reno's locally well-known Basque restaurant, Louis' Basque Corner. Louis came from the Zuberoan capital, Mauléon (Maule), a short drive north of Tardets. He emigrated to Reno at the age of nineteen, soon after the Second World War ended. He knew no English and wore a sign around his neck bearing the name and address of an uncle in Reno. When his flight from New York City to Chicago got canceled and left Louis stranded, a group of female flight attendants from Air France took him under their wing and ensured he made it to Reno. He had five dollars in his pocket, until the taxi driver who drove him to his uncle's ranch claimed the cash as his fare. An uncle had sponsored Louis' transatlantic journey but told his nephew about his new job only on the young man's arrival:

> My uncle handed me a bedroll, gave me a horse and a dog, and pointed to the two thousand sheep that I had to take up into the hills. A sheepherder! I'd never herded sheep in my life! I came from the town. I wanted to be a chef! I lasted about two weeks. My uncle was really mad at me and threatened to send me straight back to France if I didn't repay him for my passage. So I got a job bar tending at the Mapes Hotel, and by God, I paid him back. That's how I learned English! People talk a lot in American bars.

As Louis reflected upon his own sojourn from Zuberoa to the American West and the forging of his new identity as a

Basque American, he conveyed to students a strong, poignant empathy with Dominique Laxalt. Louis deeply admired him for enduring a sheepherding way of life. Although Louis returned to Zuberoa a few times in his lifetime, he knew—as Dominique Laxalt had known—that it wasn't his country anymore.

Memory, Identity, and the Changing Mythscapes of Immigration

Immigration is a major constitutive part of the American mythscape of nation-making. *Sweet Promised Land* resonates with the founding mythologies of America: it is the kind of story that conjures up images of worn-out European immigrants arriving at Ellis Island; escaping war, hunger, and persecution; and finding a home in the Promised Land. The story of the Laxalt family is a rags-to-riches Horatio Alger narrative, where the children of the sheepherding immigrant father become, through hard work and perseverance, attorney, governor, university professor, and Hall of Fame writer in just one generation. *Sweet Promised Land* is a story where European identities transform in their effort to fit in and thrive in a melting pot of identities as they become Americans. It is not just the story of a Basque American family, not even the story of Basque immigration to the United States. The memoir's enduring success is because it captures a particular era and mythscape: the American Dream and the founding narratives of the American nation. A student comment noted the book's resonance with the iconic moment of fatigued immigrants arriving Ellis Island and catching sight of the Statue of Liberty:

> Immigrants have been coming to America, "the Land of the Free," to find work, opportunity, and the freedom to choose whatever way they seek to make it. I think of the Statue of Liberty and her inscription, "Give me your tired, your poor . . ."

Much has changed about the status of immigration and the perception of immigrants in the past few decades. Walls have been erected, immigrants have been criminalized, families have been separated, and migrants have been incarcerated and deported (Boehm 2017; Douglas and Sáenz 2013). Rather than a constitutive element of national identity formation, contemporary immigration is often presented as a source of danger and contamination. Arizona's Sonoran desert has become a "land of open graves" (Léon 2015): hundreds die every year in efforts to cross the southern border as the state weaponizes the desert and forces migration routes to cross it hoping that the perils of the journey would serve as a deterrent (Cornelius 2001). Deportations and resistance to legalize immigrants are political positions that set a stark contrast between immigrant mythscapes of the past and the realities of the present. "It is sad," a student noted, "that something that was so pivotal to the foundation of the country has shifted into something so polarized." Students note these transformations as *Sweet Promised Land* prompts them to critically examine founding myths and recognize them as constructions bred and shaped by a particular epoch. As one student observed:

> There is an overwhelming amount of people who view immigrants as a threat to American society. The United States, which has often promoted this idea of being a "melting pot" with opportunities for everyone, pushes away the people it's trying to claim it supports. I would argue that the promise of a world full of opportunities no longer exists, and maybe never did, to begin with.

Sweet Promised Land is an eminently suitable pedagogical tool with which to reflect upon these transformations in the college classroom. Vaczi's Basque Culture class, which is entirely online, ends with a module that critically examines the myths and realities of immigration through students' perception of the politics of immigration. By this module, students have learned about Basque history, society, culture, and politics in a European context. Teaching *Sweet Promised Land* allows students to critically reflect on the memories, identities, myths, and narratives of not just Basque immigration, but the Constitution of the United States itself, and the impact of its founding premises on today's society. Students are asked to respond to four interrelated questions:

1. What do you think the title *Sweet Promised Land* means?

2. How has this promise changed over time? Is the US still a promised land for immigrants?

3. What title would you give to a novel about recent immigration to the US?

4. How can you relate *Sweet Promised Land* to your own family immigration story? In the following, we will present student responses to these questions.

From Biblical Origins to Capitalist Ideology: Old and New Meanings of the Promised Land

The question about the meanings of the title of the book, and how those meanings have changed since the time of the book aimed to get students to reflect about the founding ideals and narratives of their country, and to critically assess how reality might have drifted from these narratives. Student responses showed a binary conceptualization of past myths and current realities. That is how the meanings of the title *Sweet Promised Land* was seen as both "hope" and a "false hope;" as "promise of a better life" as well as "misleading promises." What some students saw as "freedom," "opportunity," and "social mobility" was identified as "American privilege" by others. Some saw *Sweet Promised Land* as "home," "authentic belonging," the "American dream," and a "melting pot." For others, the same title was "capitalistic ideology" and "a romanticized advertisement of the colonized West." Students identified the constitutive parts of the mythscape of American national formation, but they also critically identified the reverse side of those myths, showing that consciousness is changing.

In students' comments, the Promised Land is variously identified as a mythical place, a historical place, a nostalgic fantasy, and a liminal space of transformation. One student recognized the Biblical origins of the Promised Land, which resonates with Bible-inspired American founding narratives of the "city on a hill," a "beacon of hope," "American exceptionalism," and Manifest Destiny.

> "Sweet Promised Land"—the phrase, not the book—is a Biblical allusion to Canaan, the land promised by God to the Israelites. Heaven on earth. Or so I think. It's been a while since I read the Bible.
>
> "When I read the title *Sweet Promised Land*, I think that it means a safe place to be. When I read the title I think that it means that someone has found a sanctuary where they can be finally free. That the people looking for this promised land were leaving or escaping from a place that was restricting."

Many students recognized the irony in the title *Sweet Promised Land*, given that the book revolves around the struggles and difficulties of an immigrant family in an unhospitable environment (Douglass and Bilbao, 1975; Saitua 2019). Struggle and overcoming are essential tropes of mythologies of the American West and Manifest Destiny, and they resonate with founding narratives of self-reliance and rugged individualism. In this sense, the Basque sheepherder who survives and even thrives in this environment, and transforms into a different person, claims his place in American national origins. The desert landscape is eminently suitable for the liminal transformations of a rite of passage through which Europeans became Americans, a student noted:

> The harsh, unforgiving Nevadan mountains and deserts transform boys into men, immigrants from Basque countries into Americans, and Robert's mother into a magnificent family matriarch. Nevada offers a difficult promise that is worth pursuing.

Another student noted that the desert did not only transform immigrants; it transformed too as a landscape and mythscape. *Sweet Promised Land* is a witness to these transformations, and it reflects the end of an epoch:

> In contrast to Mark Twain's *Roughing It*, Robert Laxalt's *Sweet Promised Land* provides the most perceptive literature about Nevada before the Nevada Test Site and Las Vegas gave the state distinct descriptions (1957–2007). While Mark Twain published his memoir on the Nevada frontier at its height, Laxalt's book and the biography of his father, Dominique, focus on the state as it steadily approaches the end of its frontier days. Twain's comic account of the mining unrest in Virginia City contrasts with Laxalt's melancholy elegy, which centers on a gentleman and his understanding sheep.

Students recognized change, transformation, and movement as central themes of the book, culminating in the father's return to the Old Country only to find that the mythical homeland is no longer home. The in-betweenness of belonging to two places or not belonging to either one is a salient immigrant experience. A third place, students insinuated, exists in the memories of immigrants of the place they left but which no longer exists. The loss of that memory, which is constitutive of identity, is painful and fearful:

> The Sweet Promised Land concept has more to do with the idealization of the Basque Country than with the Americas. It is that eternal promise to go back to a nostalgic past, a nostalgic land full of meaning, mixed feelings, and sentimental value. And, because of this idealization, it is often difficult for the Basque sheepherders to [go] back to that land of dreams of remembrance, since going back to that desired dreamland could potentially destroy their image of that place. [It is] the fear to find everything changed, everything gone, but especially to find out as a reflection, that they themselves have changed and that they don't belong anymore to their promised motherland.

> As the book progresses, I sometimes wondered if sweet, promised land was the attitude towards the Nevada desert, and how this idea of America being a sweet, promised land was the attitude that Dominique had to have in order to have the perseverance to drive sheep in such brutally hot and cold conditions outside year-round.

The book often reminded students of their own privilege, which resonates with contemporary discourses that call for a critical reflection on positionality. One recognition of privilege is the admission that, for a nonimmigrant, it is difficult to perfectly understand the immigration experience, past or present:

> And I empathize with but can't relate to people willing to leave behind everything, travel thousands of miles, walk across rivers and mountains and geography. I've never experienced that kind of fear or urgency.

Finally, the discussion of the book prompted students to reach out to and reconnect with their own family histories of immigration. This is a particularly gratifying exercise because students get to articulate and share the origin stories of their own families. Furthermore, the sharing of family histories places students in the same mythscape, as almost everyone has a family migration story to recall. Almost always, the stories evoke the allure but also disenchantment of the American Dream.

> My personal journey is one that resonates greatly with Robert Laxalt memoir—like Laxalt, my mother was a first-generation immigrant who settled initially in California. For my mother, her driving force was a strong push for a lifetime of opportunities beyond the fate of manual labor or childbearing for her children. My father was murdered at an early age and my mother did her best to give my older brother and I the best life possible. She immigrated to this country from Guatemala and worked as a housemaid for 38 years, cleaning for others day after day with us

> by her side helping where we could in between grade school homework assignment breaks, using her toil to inspire us to do better.

Another student wrote:

> This promised land was full of dreams when my parents first migrated to America and my siblings and I stayed behind. My parents said it's nice over here, there's snow, lots of things to do, and money and food aren't a problem but when my siblings and I migrated here and lived again with our parents, it wasn't rainbows and sunshine, they had to work hard for everything they wanted and it wasn't easy because of the language barrier and culture shock that we as a family experienced. The same "there is no place like home" I never actually understood that until we migrated here. There is literally no place like home and staying here made us all homesick and just want to feel like we belong here but it's really not like that because this place is territorial and the people as well. Our skin and accent tell everybody that we are not from here.

An Over-Promise that is Under-Delivered?

What happened to the Promised Land? Most students still think that the US has freedom, opportunity, and individuality to offer, but not the ways it used to, and it no longer monopolizes that appeal. Some argued that "America may have been passed up by other countries when it comes to opportunities." Others argued in a constructivist vein that we must question whether the US "really ever was" a land of bounty, and whether the Promised Land is an "over promise that is under-delivered." Students recognized the discrepancy between the exaltation of immigration as a historical event and a founding narrative, and the perception of the very real bodies of real immigrants. They detected this discrepancy in the book, too:

> Today, there are still countries or nations that are so war-torn and full of poverty that America still looks to them as *A Sweet Promised Land.* I do not believe that the US is the same *Sweet Promised Land* for immigrants as in the book. You could already see times were changing in the story by how America lost its appeal as a land of opportunity during the mid-20th century, notably for immigrant groups like the Puerto Ricans. They had no work and were treated like a nuisance by the residents in the area.

Students identified factors such as changing immigration laws, historic events such as 9/11, a declining economy, changing social structures, the persistence of racism, the decrease of social mobility, and population growth for the changing status of the United States as a Sweet Promised Land. In other words, the Dream is still there but it is no longer idealized as it comes with caveats and strings attached:

> America for example, could be considered [a Sweet Promised Land]—being that we are so advanced in all aspects and ensure freedom for its citizens—in exchange for certain rights, gun violence, assaults and kidnappings, the violence behind politics, etc.
>
> It is still a land of opportunities but (. . .) in order to turn those opportunities into the actual reality you need to work hard and always compete.

> I would say the events of 9/11 not only transformed the country in every way but made the immigration process more difficult which probably makes the country more undesirable from an outside perspective.
>
> Upward mobility has become harder within the modern era in part because of wage theft by the upper classes as well as due to inflation.
>
> As more people come to America, fewer jobs and houses are available, and as times go, the cost of living is not something that most can afford.
>
> I think that our population has grown so much that policies had to be put into place to control population growth.

Importantly, as students discussed how the Promise changed for immigrants, they also projected their own sense of vulnerability about success and progress. Comments intimate a generation's sense of anxiety about their prospects in their country. They show that Generation Z is torn between a real sense of privilege and an equally real sense of hardship as they struggle to start a life with greater student debt, greater inflation, greater home prices, and a greater sense of insecurity than previous generations.

> I wonder if the United States was ever the Promised Land promised. That feels like marketing. But also, I'm a middle-aged white guy with unremarkably Anglo-European ancestors. I'm not very high on the promise of America these days. It doesn't feel like the place you come to for opportunity anymore, which makes me wonder to what extent it ever was. Or if it was just a place where new markets exploited labor in different ways. Despite that, I know millions of people would

> come if they could. I recognize my privilege. It's why I've had such a hard time writing this.

Student responses express a loss of confidence in their own opportunities and agency to craft the life they desire. Often, the boundaries between immigrants' prospects and students' prospects blur in the comments, and it becomes hard to tell whom students talk about, rendering themselves immigrants in their own country. Feelings of bitterness and disillusion are clearly discernible:

> I think inflation has hurt that promise in America. As living costs increase, it's very hard to get a life started.
>
> Living costs in America are becoming borderline un-survivable, depending on where you live and your socioeconomic standing, but jobs still remain available in a broader sense. I think America is a bittersweet land.
>
> Things have become extremely expensive, competitive, and unfair. Access to health care, food, insurance, convenient transportation, and more have become much more limited over the years. Racism, politics, etc. have created brokenness in America. The inequalities have made it nearly impossible for some to achieve the goals they once hoped for when arriving in the US.
>
> My grandma told me that her grandmother had heard that the streets in the early Americas were "made of gold," which is a phrase describing the boundless opportunities in this country. Although there are still many opportunities here, I think that they can be harder to find or require more personal connections to take advantage of.

Students' critical attitude to and ambiguous feelings about the promise of their country for immigrants culminate in the exercise where they are asked to creatively devise a book title for contemporary immigration. "America, on its own, isn't a promised land or an answer to humanity's problems," a student wrote. "The promise feels unfulfilled. I know I feel let down. Maybe there's a book title there?" Students' book titles reflect the duality of fiction and reality, and the elusiveness of the American Dream:

The Fact and the Dream

The Illusion of Equality and Opportunity.

Will this Hard Place be Home?

En Medio/In between

An Uncertain Sweet Land

A Broken Promise

The American Reality

The American Dream and Nightmare

Facing America

Nightmare Dressed Like a Daydream.

The American Nightmare: A Criticism of the American Dream, and What It Means to be an Immigrant in Modern America

The Bitter-Sweetland

Transplant Rejection: The Malignant Politics Controlling Immigration

Connecting Generations by Teaching *Sweet Promised Land*

Teaching *Sweet Promised Land* is not only a teaching of history to young generations; it is also uniquely positioned to help young generations express their frustrations and worldviews through critical and comparative lenses. The book thus allows an encounter of mutual learning and connection between generations of Basque Americans and American college students. In March 2023, we presented this paper at the University of Nevada, Reno, at an international conference celebrating Robert Laxalt's one hundredth birthday. The event attracted a great crowd consisting of the university community, friends and family of the Laxalts, and Basque Americans. Basque Americans enjoyed listening to how American college students read and discussed the mythscapes of their immigration; however, a certain defensiveness of the Promise was detectable. Some of our Basque American audience felt that students' perception of today's immigration as "harder," "more difficult" or "complicated" than before detracted from the resilience and hard work of previous immigrant generations—their own families. As a Basque American man told Ott after the presentation, "My father came to this country as a child of a Basque family. He did not speak any English at the beginning—and he died a very wealthy man." This comment suggests that for this man, college students today fail to perceive, despite their efforts, their privilege, and they have no real sense of hardship and difficulty. In turn, college students' comments show that they feel that their sense of precarity is not properly acknowledged by older generations, for whom the promise of the American Dream was more real. Teaching *Sweet Promised Land* opens the chance to bridge misunderstandings and be more appreciative of experiences across generations.

Bibliography

Bell, Duncan S. A. "Mythscapes: Memory, Mythology, and National Identity." *The British Journal of Sociology* 54, no. 1 (2003): 63–81.

Boehm, Deborah A. "Separated Families: Barriers to Family Reunification after Deportation." *Journal on Migration and Human Security* 5, no. 2 (2017): 401–416.

Cornelius, Wayne A. "Death at the Border: Efficacy and Unintended consequences of US Immigration Control Policy." *Population and Development Review* 27, no. 4 (2001): 661–685.

Douglas, Karen Manges, and Rogelio Sáenz. "The Criminalization of Immigrants & the Immigration-Industrial Complex." *Daedalus* 142, no. 3 (2013): 199-227.

Douglass, William A. and Jon Bilbao. *Amerikanuak*. Reno: University of Nevada Press, 1975.

Léon, Jason de. *The Land of Open Graves: Living and Dying on the Migrant Trail.* Berkeley: University of California Press, 2015.

Ott, Sandra. "*Indarra*: Some Reflections on a Basque Concept." In *Honour and Grace*, edited by John Peristiany and Julian Pitt-Rivers, 193–214. Cambridge: Cambridge University Press.

Ott, Sandra. *The Circle of Mountains: A Basque Shepherding Community*. Reno: University of Nevada Press, 1993.

Ott, Sandra. *War, Judgment and Memory in the Basque Borderlands, 1914–1945*. Reno: University of Nevada Press, 2008.

Saitua, Iker. *Basque Immigrants and Nevada's Sheep Industry: Geopolitics and the Making of an Agricultural Workforce, 1880–1954*. Reno: University of Nevada Press, 2019.

Notes

1 Professor Ott and her students remain grateful to the Basque librarian, Iñaki Arrieta Baro, for generously enabling them to use material culture held in the archives of the Jon Bilbao Basque Library and Special Collections.

2 See Sandra Ott, *War, Judgment and Memory in the Basque Borderlands, 1914–1945* (Reno: University of Nevada Press, 2008), especially chapter three, "Basques in the Great War."

3 I am unable to locate the student, who took the class eighteen years ago, and have therefore not cited her by name. For an overview of the concept of *indarra,* see Sandra Ott, *The Circle of Mountains: A Basque Shepherding Community*. (Reno: University of Nevada Press, 1993) and Sandra Ott, "*Indarra*: A Basque

Concept," in John Peristiany and Julian Pitt-Rivers, *Honor and Grace*. (Cambridge, UK: Cambridge University Press, 1981), 193–214.

4 These are students' observations about the meaning of "home."

Place and Identity in Robert Laxalt's Basque Family Trilogy[1]

by David Rio

Literary scholars have long dedicated significant attention to the interplay among place, space, and characters. Certainly, some perspectives still show some negative prejudices toward place and region as relevant critical categories, suggesting that their minor interest is because of their connection to local writing and literature of merely regional interest. Thus, for example, in 1988 *The Columbia Literary History of the United States* included an essay entitled "Regionalism: A Diminished Thing," in which its author (James M. Cox) defined *regionalism* as "a subordinate form of realism."[2] Other authors have pointed out the lack of proper terms to label some issues related to place. Gary Snyder, for instance, has noted that "we have the terms *enculturation* and *acculturation*, but nothing to describe the process of becoming placed or re-placed."[3] Nevertheless, increasing attention is being paid to the interconnectedness of identity, space, and place, emphasizing the complex process of negotiating one's place in particular cultural, social, and physical spaces. For instance, Michael Kowalewski has argued that place is "one of the central impulses in American literature," with authors evoking "a spirit of place" that "involve[s] more than simply background color or a little local seasoning."[4] The expansion of globalization and transnational studies and approaches in an international context may have served to promote particular modes of reading whereby the cosmopolitan dimension of the texts is emphasized, whereas the specifics of place are diminished. However, as Sten Pultz Moslund has noted, "the corporal body, locality, place, and experience of physical emplacement [. . .] continue to matter, in literature, too, even in these times of flux, uprooting, and great speeds of mobility."[5] In fact, in the past few decades scholars have commonly agreed that spatiality has achieved increasing prominence in literary studies. For example, Jeremy Wells has underlined the growing "recognition of the ways in which *place* transforms other categories of identity and shapes different forms of cultural recognition."[6] Similarly, Robert T. Tally has explained that "in recent years the spatial turn in literary and cultural studies has opened up new ways of looking at the interactions among writers, readers, texts, and places."[7] This theoretical framework becomes very useful to explore Robert Laxalt's writing because most of his works illustrate his preoccupation with place and its impact on identity, as exemplified by his Basque family trilogy.

In the spring of 1995, during my first visit to the University of Nevada, Reno, I had the enormous privilege of meeting Robert Laxalt, an author whose work had inspired my then-incipient research on Basque American literature. At that time, Laxalt was teaching a graduate course at the Reynolds School of Journalism focused on American authors whose writing was deeply connected to journalism (Jack London, Mark Twain, Ernest Hemingway, and a few others). I received an invitation to visit some of his classes, and after his first class, a discussion of Hemingway's *The Old Man and the Sea*, I was aware of Laxalt's emphasis on place as one of the key factors in a writer's work. Thus, he underscored the interaction between the main character of Hemingway's novella, Santiago, and the sea and its creatures. In particular, Laxalt underlined the power of the sea to shape Santiago's identity. While he and his students were discussing the role of the sea in Hemingway's book, inevitably I started thinking about the overwhelming impact of place on most of Laxalt's works. In fact, since the publication of his first book, *The Violent Land: Tales the Old Timers Tell About Nevada* (1953), a collection of sixteen short stories set in Nevada in the mid-nineteenth century, place became a key concern for Laxalt. Obviously, his second book, the highly acclaimed memoir *Sweet Promised Land* (1957), would be one of the most illustrative examples of the prominent role played by place in Laxalt's literary career. These two books were followed by a long list of titles in which a character's response to a particular place serves to convey a sense of self. Even the titles of many of these books already seem to anticipate the central function of place in Laxalt's works. Thus, many of these titles are connected somehow to place; see, for example, titles such as *A Man in the Wheatfield* (1964), *Nevada* (1970), *In a Hundred Graves: A Basque Portrait* (1972), *Nevada: A History* (1977), *A Cup of Tea in Pamplona* (1977), *A Time We Knew: Images of Yesterday in the Basque Homeland* (1990), *A Private War: An American Code Officer in the Belgian Congo* (1998), or *The Land of My Fathers: A Son's Return to the Basque Country* (1999). This dominant presence of place in Laxalt's work also extends to his semiautobiographic Basque family trilogy, consisting of *The Basque Hotel* (1989), *Child of the Holy Ghost* (1992), and *The Governor's Mansion* (1994). Although Laxalt himself told me, in an interview in 1997, that family was the most important common thread in these three novels,[8] in this essay I argue that Laxalt's concern with the main characters' subjective perceptions of geographical space play a pivotal role in the construction of their identities throughout the whole trilogy. The novels show Laxalt's exploration of the interconnection between place and identity, addressing issues such as alienation, nostalgia, rootedness, adjustment, dislocation, and restlessness.

In *The Basque Hotel*, the first volume of the trilogy, place stands out since the very beginning of the novel, as illustrated by its first sentence: "Along the length of Main Street, the business people of Carson City had come out to sweep the sidewalks in front of their shops and stores and little hotels."[9] In his characteristic spare and lean prose, Laxalt introduces the readers to the setting of his novel, Carson City, Nevada, in the early 1930s, offering a panoramic perspective of the place where the protagonist lives: the main street of the smallest capital in the United States at that time. Only one page later, the reference to the "little hotels" becomes more specific when two particular hotels are mentioned: the Columbo Hotel, owned by an Italian immigrant, and the Basque Hotel, the place where Pete and his family live. Thus, the reader notices that place is soon associated with ethnicity and, implicitly, to class. Main Street is portrayed not as a fancy area to live but as a place to work where immigrants have to make a living and adjust to American society.

Pete's home, the Basque Hotel, works as an iconic significant place in Laxalt's novel. For Pete, this hotel challenges notions of home and domestic life because it is a setting where the private sphere coexists with the public dimension. He experiences in a peculiar environment varying forms of freedom and constraint that have a relevant impact on his adolescent years. The hotel should be regarded not as a passive or an ornamental backdrop for Pete's coming-of-age process, but as a major component of his quest for identity. On the one hand, the hotel provides him with a sense of home, domestic life, comfort, stability, and protection. Thus, the hotel is the place where he will recover from his rheumatic fever with the support and supervision of his family and friends. In the hotel, Pete will also learn about this ethnic identity, about his family's past in the Basque Country, and about their early immigrant years in America. On the other hand, living in a hotel implies a constant interaction with the outside world and the recurrent intrusion of public life into the domestic realm. As Emma Short has claimed, "characterized by impermanence in the constant coming and going of its guests and yet underpinned by the routine and order of the work of the hotel staff, it is a space that at once exemplifies the flux and chaos of modernity in the early twentieth century, as well as the rationalization of space that was taking place during the same period."[10] In Laxalt's novel, for example, safety, stability, order, and privacy are challenged by the regular visits of the Prohibition agents who do not only come for dinner but also try to search the place for alcoholic spirits. In this sense, it is also worth emphasizing that the hotel where Pete grows up is not a regular hotel but a Basque hotel. This Basqueness adds a particular dimension to Pete's domestic space because it identifies his dwellers not just with the Other (with a non-Anglo group of immigrants) but also with a community who lived at the margins of the law because of their attitude toward Prohibition. As Richard H. Lane has observed, "Basques were accused of being the major bootleggers during prohibition, but were scarcely the only ones active in this largely tolerated illegality."[11] In Laxalt's novel, the hotel is a business already marked by the past of his previous owner, who was sent to prison for bootlegging, and the need to continue selling alcohol to avoid bankruptcy does not help Pete's family achieve a respectable identity. As Pete's father states in the novel, "I can't figure this country out. [. . .] If you don't serve people booze, you go broke. And if you do serve it, you get into trouble. [. . .] If giving people a little wine for dinner and a couple shots of whiskey beforehand is being a bootlegger, then I guess we are bootleggers."[12] Laxalt himself wrote in his memoir *Travels with My Royal* about the shame that was inflicted on his family because their hotel was associated with bootlegging: "Being bootleggers put us in a lower social standing, though I never could make the distinction between our serving whiskey and those who bought it—including the occupants of the Governor's Mansion and the opulent homes of supreme court justices. We paid the penalty for it when our schoolmates called us bootleggers in accusatory tones that were a mark of shame."[13]

In Laxalt's novel only one guest is mentioned: Tristant, a Basque sheepherder. He plays a secondary role in Pete's story, but it is implicit that the hotel acquires a different meaning for this character. For Tristant, the hotel is not the site of illegal activities by a group of immigrants; it means a home away from home, the traditional meaning of these boardinghouses for many Basque immigrants.[14] The hotel brings Tristant a temporary break from his harsh life as a sheepherder in the hills and a way to reconnect with a familiar language, culture, and cuisine. Pete is aware of the rewards that are available to Tristant while staying at the Basque hotel, away from the austere life in the mountains, including apparently insignificant things such as having cereal and milk for breakfast. However, he teases the sheepherder, pretending to take for himself the last box of cornflakes left, although in the end he lets Tristant get the box and enjoy his breakfast. Significantly enough, the fact that both of them are Basque does not seem to create a particular bond between these characters, as illustrated by Tristant's mumbling "Good morning" in Basque and Pete answering in English. Pete does not reject his ethnic heritage, but his relationship with Tristant in the Basque hotel epitomizes his inability as a child to understand the true dimension and implications of this heritage.

The Basque hotel is not the only example in the novel of the protagonist's complex navigation of place and space during his growing-up years in Carson City. In fact, the novel includes several public places that are often associated to spaces of power, such as the school, the Capitol, and the church. These places do not offer comfort to Pete, but they become sites of tension and conflict that in a way contribute to Pete's maturity and self-knowledge. For example, the school works as a space of power where those who are different from mainstream society have to cope with fear, shame, and prejudice. Pete, for example, experiences bullying because his Basque ethnicity associates him with socially despised activities such as bootlegging and sheepherding. Ethnic prejudice has much worse consequences for his Native American friend Romy, who becomes the victim of physical violence by other schoolmates under the passive observance of the principal.

Another public space that has an important impact on Pete's maturation is the Capitol, one of the main symbols of political power in Carson City. This time, it is a place not for shame or prejudice but revenge: Pete chooses the Capitol as the site for his childish revenge against the Prohibition agents (Prohis); this is illustrated by his illegally entering this building at night with his friend Tony and running through its corridors with leather heels and brass taps. In a way, it is a misguided revenge because the Prohis represent federal authority, whereas the Capitol represents the state government, but the main point for Pete is that the Capitol is a symbol of authority. His negotiation across this physical and social space certainly appears intertwined with the formation of his identity. Significantly enough, this episode ends with Pete ruminating about the meaning of this blow against authority: "He sensed now that vengeance was a part of his makeup that he could do nothing about, but he was not sure whether he liked that. [. . .] Somewhere within Pete, he felt a vague awareness of lessons learned and a premonition that he was beginning to discover his world."[15]

Later in the novel Pete will have to endure tensions, conflict, and shame at another public space related to power, the church. One of the major rituals associated with this site, the Mass, will be a major source of anxiety for Pete when he faces the need to confess to Father O'Malley his first sexual experience. The burden of guilt and fear brings confusion to Pete's mind and the confession after the Mass will open Father O'Malley's eyes to the child's improbable future as a priest. Another Mass, almost at the end of the novel, brings more shame to Pete because of his uncle Joanes's attitude in the church. He not only insists on saying his prayers in a foreign language, but he also asks the man in charge of the collection plate for change. Once again, Pete's family and, in particular, their ethnic identity, become a source of shame for Pete in a public space. In fact, because of this shame he even pretends unsuccessfully that "Uncle Joanes did not belong to their family."[16]

Open natural spaces around Carson City also play an important role in the novel because Pete's subjective perceptions of these geographical areas are deeply connected with the construction of his identity. Thus, for example, when Pete starts his expedition into the woods in the midst of winter, he sees himself as a pioneer bound to face the unknown in order to get a Christmas tree: "Beyond the poplars was the unknown. Behind him was the certainty of home and shelter. [. . .] *To be afraid of a thing and yet to do it is what makes the prettiest kind of man.*[17] Picturing the explorers who must have repeated the same words, Pete steeled himself and set out resolutely."[18] This risky expedition responds to Pete's intent to avoid alienation from "his friends who live in real houses instead of a hotel [and] talked about their Christmas trees."[19] Once again Pete is placed in an awkward situation, in a liminal position where American standards clash with Basque traditions.

In the second part of the novel, Pete's trip to the mountains with his father and brothers helps him not only to learn about the true nature of the sheepherder's life but also to become closer to his father, who guides him through a series of rites of passage. Life in contact with nature provides Pete with self-knowledge and a gradual awareness about his family identity and work. However, he is not ready to share all this new knowledge because he fears rejection and anticipates his friends' inability to accept common activities in a sheepherder's life: "They would not understand and he would be too ashamed to tell them of the things that went on a sheepcamp."[20]

The power of placial experiences in Laxalt's novel may be also noticed in the radical change that leads Pete's family to sell the hotel and buy a house in the respectable part of Carson City: "They had moved only six blocks away from the little house, but it might as well have been six hundred miles."[21] Pete's new residence serves Laxalt to explore the real meaning of home and the way in which one's identity may be attached to a particular place. The new house is described as an intimidating space because of its size. However, Pete's uneasiness about this place is linked to their new neighborhood, consisting of wealthy people who at the beginning refuse to socialize with his family because of their Basque origin and the negative connotations associated with it. The novel shows how accepted notions of home and domestic life seem not to fit into the new house because of this intimidating neighborhood. In fact, Pete feels out of place here, as illustrated by his frustrated attempt to escape from his house and return to the old hotel. In the end, the novel emphasizes the malleability of place and the unstable condition of tropes such as home. After all, as Doreen Massey has claimed, "the identities of place are always unfixed, contested, and multiple."[22] Thus, in the second part of the novel the reader observes how Pete gradually feels at home in the new neighborhood, but he loses his connection to the hotel and its regular visitors. Pete's break with his old world is exemplified by an encounter with one of his former friends, a drunkard called Buckshot, who blames Pete and his family for having bought the new house with the money he spent at the hotel. This episode definitely embodies Pete's loss of his ties with the old hotel and its neighborhood and his acceptance of his belonging to a new social, economic, and cultural environment: "In one instant, Buckshot had wrecked all of Pete's waking dreams of Main Street. Pete wanted desperately to go home, and home was no longer the little hotel, and never would be again."[23] This disengagement of his old identity seems to be epitomized by the accidental burning of the old hotel at the end of the novel. The disappearance of this place may be regarded as a symbol not only of the transformation of Carson City but also of Pete's own growth and his break with the past. However, the burning of the hotel also gives birth to "a rush of unexpected recollections" flooding over Pete. Significantly enough, he moves away from those residents and tourists who, while witnessing the fire, link the burning of the hotel with progress and change for Carson City. In this way, Laxalt hints that the connection between memory and place cannot be so easily broken and, in fact, this issue plays a major role in *Child of the Holy Ghost*, the second novel of his family trilogy.

In *Child of the Holy Ghost* Laxalt offers another insightful examination of the interaction between place and identity, tracing the events that impelled Pete's parents to leave the Basque Country and settle in the American West. This novel is a prequel to *The Basque Hotel*, in which Laxalt has already introduced Pete's emerging awareness about his family connection with a foreign land. It was still a very vague knowledge through his mother's stories and pictures because, after all, "the idea of relatives in a foreign land was new to Pete. It was something that he would have to think about later."[24] Thus, the second novel of the trilogy opens with Pete, now an adult and the narrator of the story, visiting the Basque Country "to learn about the ways of the Basques in their ancestral villages."[25] Pete feels that he will not be able to know the true nature of Basque identity until he is able to see the Basques in their own land: "I already knew about how immigrant Basques lived and thought in the United States, but there had always been something missing, and that something was how they lived and thought in their natural element."[26] Once again, Laxalt emphasizes the major role played by the land in shaping one's character. The story of Pete's trip to the Basque Country soon becomes an immersion not only into a traditional way of life in an ancient region but also into a family secret: Pete's mother, Maitia, was born illegitimate, "a Child of the Holy Ghost." This particular fact is regarded as irrelevant from an American perspective ("Middle Ages nonsense").[27] However, it is regarded as a key factor in some places of the Basque Country, affecting such issues as inheritance patterns, pride of name, and family honor.

From the very beginning of the novel, geographical determinism and characters' negotiations within and across physical and cultural spaces take center stage. The first part of this novel is set mainly in the lowlands of the French Basque Country, in Donibane (Basse Navarre/Benafarroa), Maitia's hometown. The sharp contrast that is established between the Basques living in this area and those dwelling in the province of Pete's father (Zuberoa) in the high mountains of the Pyrenees is worth mentioning. Place again plays a prominent role in the process of identity configuration, even within the same ethnic group. We learn, for example, that in the highlands "premature bedding and illegitimacy are of no moment. They are the facts of life and accepted as that. The high-mountain Basques tell the truth down to the last comma, and they are sticklers for accuracy."[28] On the contrary, the lowlanders in

Basse Navarre are portrayed as an extremely close community where one's identity is based on tradition and family honor. In these villages, scandals and secrets should be not shared with outsiders, and the break of ancient moral and religious patterns implies the loss of respectability and one's social identity in the eyes of the community. Tradition becomes more important than the law, and those who challenge it face public condemnation, as happens with the mothers of illegitimate children. The power of tradition is symbolized in the novel by the farmhouse of Maitia's grandfather (Garat), built in 1454. It is a very solid building that has endured the passage of time with scarcely any change and that promises to remain in a similar shape in the near future: "another century will have no more effect upon it than the last five have."[29] However, the fortress stone of the house shows its fragility when its inhabitants suffer public condemnation from the villagers because of Maitia's birth as an illegitimate child. The weight of tradition and moral taboos overcomes the strength of the house, as illustrated by the *galarrotza*,[30] the noisy act of censure by the village for the violation of the moral code: "there came an intruder whose entry was not to be denied by stone and iron and oak."[31] The powerful physical dimension symbolized by the house surrenders to social and moral restrictions that have remained unchangeable through centuries. Although the farmhouse remains, Maitia's family inevitably loses its good name, its former respectable social identity.

In the second part of *Child of the Holy Ghost,* the high mountains of Zuberoa replace Basse Navarre as the main location of the novel as we learn how the peaceful life of Pete's father (Petya) as a sheepherder there is shattered by his chance observation of a murder by a smuggler. This incident will force him to leave his loved land because he realizes that, because he witnessed a murder, his life is in danger. His destiny will be the United States, a country that works in the novel as a land of refuge, not as a country freely chosen by an individual searching for prosperity. Petya's travel to America includes two stops, the first one in Donibane and the second one in Bordeaux, at a hotel called Amerika, a very proper name for such a hotel because it was the place where young Basques were recruited to become sheepherders in the United States. The hotel embodies a liminal situation for these Basques, who are already away from home but still on their way to America. This borderline status is a source of discomfort for these Basques, who feel out of place in this setting. It is a complete new experience for them, and their fear of the unknown becomes highly noticeable: "None of them had been more than ten miles away from their villages in their lives. [. . .] And they showed it. They were scared to death."[32]

Parts III and IV of *Child of the Holy Ghost* alternate between the two storylines in the novel: that of Maitia's ordeals as an illegitimate child and that of Petya's forced immigration to America. This alternation gives birth to two rotating settings: the ancestral village of Donibane, where Maitia has to deal with injustice and prejudice, and Nevada, where Petya will face perils and loneliness in the desert and the city temptations in Reno. The novel emphasizes the increasing alienation of Maitia from her home village, a place where in the end she will even be deprived of her family inheritance, losing the house and the land. The loss of her physical place in Donibane means for her the break of her last ties with this village, the end of her identity in this community. Therefore, it is no wonder that she decides to leave Donibane, stating explicitly that she no longer wishes to see this village again. Alienation also defines Petya's life in America, where he has found a refuge but not a true home. He is unable to identify himself with a land that has not provided him with success and that remains almost completely unknown to him: "What I know of America is no more than a coyote knows."[33] His wish to return to the

Basque Country after five years of maddening loneliness and a harsh life as a sheepherder in the Nevada desert and hills is stopped only by his employer, Laborde. He agrees to make Petya a business partner if he overcomes the temptation to waste his wages in Reno, a city traditionally associated with gambling, prostitution, and vice. Petya's success in defeating the city temptations is linked in the novel to a place that serves as a refuge for the young sheepherders: a Basque hotel. Once again, Laxalt introduces the motif of the Basque hotel in America as a place where the Basque immigrants may feel at home, emphasizing in this novel its role of shelter for the young sheepherders who need protection from the devastating temptations of a city such as Reno, in "a country of strangers, country of wolves."[34]

In the epilogue, Laxalt unites the stories of Maitia and Petya, introducing several places that play a powerful symbolic role in their lives. Thus, Maitia will follow Petya's steps on her way to America to meet her ill brother Michel. In fact, she stops at the same hotel in Bordeaux where Pete stayed before leaving for the United States. Her arrival in America means "her emancipation from the stigma she had borne since the night she had been born a Child of the Holy Ghost."[35] In addition, it is no wonder that this feeling of emancipation is connected in the novel to her view of the Statue of Liberty, a universal icon of freedom in the broadest sense. In Reno, Maitia goes to the same Basque hotel where Petya had overcome the temptations of this city, and their meeting takes place at a hospital there, St. Mary's. The fact that Maitia and Petya see each other for the first time at a hospital has symbolic connotations because both characters are immersed in a process of healing from particular personal traumas Although Maitia's brother dies at this hospital, this place has obvious positive implications for Maitia as it becomes the starting point of her love relationship with

Petya. The last three pages of the book move the story back to the Basque Country, a place that becomes a site of justice, punishment, and vindication. Pete and his father, while visiting the high Pyrenees, learn that the smuggler chieftain who had threatened Petya's life was in the end killed by members of his own band. This smuggler is not the only one paying for past crimes and injustice: the town of Donibane, represented by its mayor, will be also publicly censured by Pete's brother (Leon) when he is invited to visit the village after winning the governorship of Nevada. Leon's vengeful speech denouncing the town's mistreatment of his mother and grandmother is written by Pete himself. Thus, Donibane becomes in the end a site of revenge and retaliation. This critical view of Donibane may surprise readers familiar with other books by Laxalt set in the Basque Country, which usually portray this region and its inhabitants from a positive perspective, with *A Cup of Tea in Pamplona* perhaps the only other exception. Regarding this, Laxalt himself stated the following: "*Child of the Holy Ghost* was written because I was really triggered by what happened to my mother there. I genuinely felt it. I didn't try to portray the village as cruel. It was just the way things were. [. . .] I love the Basque Country and the Basque people, but that does not deny me the right to say when they're wrong. Otherwise I couldn't be honest."[36] Nevertheless, the end of the novel also shows that, despite the injustice, ignominy, and discrimination Maitia suffered in Donibane, she cannot get rid of her affection for her homeland. She will refuse to return to the Basque Country, but at the end of her life her previous rejection of her hometown at the time she left for America is replaced by her love and longing for Donibane and her family house there: "I want so much to go back and see those beautiful little corners of my valley again. [. . .] My house and my land lie just up this pretty lane that passes the ramparts."[37]

The last volume of the trilogy, *The Governor's Mansion*, focuses on the impact of politics on Pete's family, portraying both the rewards that his brother's political success (Leon is elected as the Nevada governor) brings to the whole family and the high price to be paid for this success: the sacrifice of private life. Again, in this story, place takes center stage from the novel's beginning, as exemplified by the description of the Governor's Mansion provided by Pete in the first paragraph: "I drove past the Governor's Mansion that day. Afterwards, I wondered why I had. That imposing white edifice was not a curiosity for me. Living in the same part of the town, I had seen it so many times that I did not see it anymore. It was just a white space in the landscape."[38] The novel emphasizes the contrast between the powerful physical presence of this building and its minor role in the narrator's view. Pete's neglect of the building seems to be related to its condition of temporary residence for politicians who do not stay around "long enough to give the place a personality."[39] This idea already anticipates one of the main topics of the novel, the ephemeral condition of political life and its rewards, a subject that will be evoked again at the end of the book.

Together with the Governor's Mansion, the most relevant and symbolic building in the novel is the old family house in Carson City, where Leon's parents still live. The house appears to be a hybrid building because it resembles other houses in the neighborhood, but it differs from the others around it both physically (it was constructed in the style of Basque farmhouses) and socially (its dwellers do not observe some norms of American behavior, for example, the habit of receiving frequent guests). This hybrid nature of the house symbolizes the blended identity of the family, which has adjusted to modern American ways but is also proud of its ancient Basque values. The house plays a traditional role, one that David Sibley defines in the following way: "a source of comfort in a world otherwise replete with tension and conflict, and the only environment in which individuals can function as autonomous agents."[40] The house represents for the Indarts a sphere of safety, stability, and refuge, and because of that it becomes their main gathering place. The family house and their Friday lunches there epitomize the renewal of their ties with their immigrant past and their ethnic identity: "'As Leon said, 'It's like going back to the womb.' There, we had done most of our growing up, the house had been a fortress against the world. This is something the children of immigrants all know, or at least knew when it was not fashionable to be the children of immigrants."[41] Therefore, the house is chosen by the Indarts as their headquarters during Leon's electoral campaigns. During election nights, the hybrid condition of the house becomes more noticeable because outsiders (journalists, campaign workers and supporters, etc.) inevitably disrupt the privacy of the Indarts, which is mainly preserved by the candidate's mother. The Indarts' immersion in the public sphere interplays with the Basque passion for privacy, as shown by the fact that during election nights the house welcomes many visitors, but certain parts of the house—for example, the bedrooms—remain off limits to anyone not in the family. Similarly, the family house illustrates the intermingling of truth and lies when politics intrude upon the Indarts' lives. The house symbolizes a haven of truth for the candidate and his family ("truth had always been spoken here in times of big decisions—college and war and career"),[42] but it cannot escape from the impact of the artificial realm of political campaigns, a field where "truth was the rarest commodity."[43]

The novel also depicts the turmoil of the political world, focusing on Las Vegas as the major site of conflict and rivalry between the two main parties involved in Nevada elections. It is a city of hoodlums, tycoons, hit men, and hookers, where each party uses a casino as its major site of operations. Politics is compared with a medieval war, as illustrated by the way in which the main headquarters of each party in Las Vegas is described: "The Desert Inn was our fortress. [. . .] A mile away down the Strip, Governor Dean Cooper and his campaign team occupied another fortress, called the Sands. In an election year when everyone was running for everything, candidates for lesser offices occupied the lesser hotels. The arrangement was very much like castles in Spain, occupied by local monarchs."[44] The physical connection between the casinos and the political sphere enhances the materialistic dimension of politics, and it seems to imply that the results of political matters, including elections, are difficult to predict. In fact, the uncertain side of elections is epitomized by the failure of Leon's race for the US Senate and, in particular, by election night when "the tide was to turn three times from loss to victory to loss to victory."[45]

In contraposition to the materialistic, greedy, and artificial world of Las Vegas, the novel introduces the mountains that surround Carson City as a natural and pristine environment where both brothers renew their ties with their immigrant past, sharing memories with his father of the sheepherding days. The Sierra allows the Indarts not only to reinforce their ethnic identity through common past experiences but also to escape from their present notoriety and the turmoil of the political world. As Richard W. Etulain has claimed, "they are refreshed through their Basque traditions, cleansed from the wheeling and dealing that even invades their family home in Carson City. The clean, restorative Sierra function as do the Pyrenees in Hemingway's *The Sun Also Rises*. The alpine settings wash away the grey grime of Las Vegas and Paris, respectively."[46]

At the end of the novel it is hinted that Leon, after his first defeat in the race for the US Senate, will run again, and this time he will be successful. However, his brother Pete will refuse to continue working with him because of his disenchantment with the world of politics, a world that has deprived him of his personal identity. His dreams and personal aspirations have been relegated to second place in order to give priority to his brother's political career and to the family unity and success. To show the ephemeral condition of political glory and recognition, Laxalt will use an oneiric reference, a dream by the narrator in which the family house again plays a prominent role. In fact, in this dream Pete returns to the place where the house used to be located in Carson City to discover that nobody there remembers either the house or his family's name: "*No house of that name was ever here.* [. . .] *No one by that name ever lived here.*"[47]

Overall, Robert Laxalt's Basque family trilogy exemplifies the powerful influence of place in the construction of one's identity at different levels: personal, ethnic, family. Laxalt shows his gift of conveying a sense of place, emphasizing place as a form inherent to human identity, a central concern in his literary career. His characters respond to a variety of places, experiencing connection, alienation, or mixed feelings with particular physical, social, and cultural spaces. The three novels illustrate the problematic interconnection between individual and groups with the spatial realm, highlighting an awareness of place as a quintessential feature in human identity.

Bibliography

Cox, James M. "Regionalism: A Diminished Thing." In *The Columbia Literary History of the United States*, ed. Emory Elliott, 761–784. New York: Columbia University Press, 1988.

Echeverria, Jeronima. *Home Away from Home: A History of Basque Boardinghouses*. Reno: University of Nevada Press, 1999.

Etulain, Richard W. "Robert Laxalt: Basque Writer of the American West." In *Portraits of Basques in the New World*, eds. Richard W. Etulain and Jeronima Echeverria. Reno: University of Nevada Press, 1999.

Hemingway, Ernest. *The Old Man and the Sea*. New York: Scribner's, 1952.

Kowalewski, Michael. "Contemporary Regionalism." In *A Companion to the Regional Literatures of America*, ed. Charles L. Crow, 7–24. Malden, MA: Walden, 2003.

Lane, Richard H. "Trouble in the Sweet Promised Land: Basques in the Early 20th Century Northeastern Nevada." In *Anglo-American Contributions to Basque Studies: Essays in Honor of Jon Bilbao*, ed. William A. Douglass, Richard W. Etulain, and William H. Jacobsen, Jr., 33–41. Reno: Desert Research Institute, 1977.

Laxalt, Robert. *A Cup of Tea in Pamplona*. Reno: University of Nevada Press, 1985.

____. *A Man in the Wheatfield*. New York: Harper & Row, 1964.

____. *A Private War: An American Code Officer in the Belgian Congo*. Reno: University of Nevada Press, 1998.

____. *A Time We Knew: Images of Yesterday in the Homeland*. With photographs by William A. Allard. Reno: University of Nevada Press, 1990.

____. *Child of the Holy Ghost*. Reno: University of Nevada Press, 1992.

____. *In a Hundred Graves: A Basque Portrait*. Reno: University of Nevada Press, 1972.

____. *Nevada*. New York: Coward-Mcann, Inc., 1970.

____. *Nevada: A History*. New York: Norton, 1977.

____. *Sweet Promised Land*. New York: Harper, 1957.

____. *The Basque Hotel*. Reno: University of Nevada Press, 1989.

____. *The Governor's Mansion*. Reno: University of Nevada Press, 1994.

____. *The Land of My Fathers. A Son's Return to the Basque Country*. Reno: University of Nevada Press, 1999.

____. *The Violent Land: Tales the Old Timers Tell About Nevada*. Reno: Nevada Publishing Co., 1953.

____. *Travels with My Royal: A Memoir of the Writing Life*. Reno: University of Nevada Press, 2001.

Massey, Doreen. *Space, Place, and Gender*. Cambridge: Polity Press, 1994.

Moslund, Sten Pultz. "The Presencing of Place in Literature: Toward an Embodied Topopoetic Mode of Reading." In *Geocritical Explorations: Space, Place, and Mapping in Literary and Cultural*

Studies, ed. Robert T. Tally, 29–43. New York: Palgrave Macmillan, 2011.

Río, David, "A Basque Voice in the Promised Land: An Interview with Robert Laxalt," *REDEN (Revista Española de Estudios Norteamericanos)* 12 (1996): 125–130.

____. "A Clean Writer: An Interview with Robert Laxalt," *Revista de Estudios Norteamericanos*, 5 (1997): 21–27.

Short, Emma. *Mobility and the Hotel in Modern Literature: Passing Through*. Berlin: Springer, 2019.

Sibley, David. *Geographies of Exclusion: Society and Difference in the West*. New York: Routledge, 1995.

Snyder, Gary. *The Practice of the Wild*. With a New Preface by the Author. Berkeley, CA: Counterpoint Press, 2010.

Tally, Robert T., ed. *Geocritical Explorations: Space, Place, and Mapping in Literary and Cultural Studies*. New York: Palgrave Macmillan, 2011.

Wells, Jeremy. "The Arrival of Regions: *The Blackwell Companion to the Regional Literatures of America*," *Western American Literature* 41.2 (Summer 2006): 202–211.

Notes

1 I am indebted to the Basque government (IT1565-22) for funding the research carried out for this essay.

2 James M. Cox, "Regionalism: A Diminished Thing," in *The Columbia Literary History of the United States*, ed. Emory Elliott (New York: Columbia University Press, 1988), 761–784.

3 Gary Snyder, *The Practice of the Wild* (Berkeley, CA: Counterpoint Press, 2010), 27.

4 Michael Kowalewski, "Contemporary Regionalism," in *A Companion to the Regional Literatures of America*, ed. Charles L. Crow (Malden, MA: Walden, 2003), 7.

5 Sten Pultz Moslund, "The Presencing of Place in Literature: Toward an Embodied Topopoetic Mode of Reading," in *Geocritical Explorations: Space, Place, and Mapping in Literary and Cultural Studies*, ed. Robert T. Tally (New York: Palgrave Macmillan, 2011), 30.

6 Jeremy Wells, "The Arrival of Regions: *The Blackwell Companion to the Regional Literatures of America*," *Western American Literature* 41.2 (Summer 2006), 203.

7 Robert T. Tally, ed. *Geocritical Explorations* (back cover).

8 David Río, "A Clean Writer: An Interview with Robert Laxalt," *Revista de Estudios Norteamericanos*, 5 (1997), 26.

9 Robert Laxalt, *The Basque Hotel* (Reno: University of Nevada Press, 1989), 3.

10 Emma Short, *Mobility and the Hotel in Modern Literature: Passing Through* (Berlin: Springer, 2019), 1.

11 Richard H. Lane, "Trouble in the Sweet Promised Land: Basques in the Early 20th Century Northeastern Nevada," in *Anglo-American Contributions to Basque Studies: Essays in Honor of Jon Bilbao*, ed. William A. Douglass, Richard W. Etulain and William H. Jacobsen Jr. (Reno: Desert Research Institute, 1977), 39.

12 Laxalt, *The Basque Hotel*, 36.

13 *Travels with My Royal: A Memoir of the Writing Life* (Reno: University of Nevada Press, 2001), 4.

14 See Jeronima Echeverria's *Home Away from Home: A History of Basque Boardinghouses* (Reno: University of Nevada Press, 1999).

15 Laxalt, *The Basque Hotel*, 37.

16 Laxalt, *The Basque Hotel*, 107.

17 Italics in the original text.

18 Laxalt, *The Basque Hotel*, 41.

19 Laxalt, *The Basque Hotel*, 42.

20 Laxalt, *The Basque Hotel*, 118.

21 Laxalt, *The Basque Hotel*, 64.

22 Doreen Massey, *Space, Place, and Gender* (Cambridge: Polity Press, 1994), 5.

23 Laxalt, *The Basque Hotel*, 73.

24 Laxalt, *The Basque Hotel*, 57.

25 Robert Laxalt, *Child of the Holy Ghost* (Reno: University of Nevada Press, 1992), 3.

26 Laxalt, *Child, 3.*

27 Laxalt, *Child,* 5.

28 Laxalt, *Child,* 7.
29 Laxalt, *Child,* 12.
30 Italics in the original text.
31 Laxalt, *Child of the Holy Ghost*, 31.
32 Laxalt, *Child,* 64.
33 Laxalt, *Child,* 125.
34 Laxalt, *Child,* 138.
35 Laxalt, *Child,* 150.
36 David Rio, "A Basque Voice in the Promised Land: An Interview with Robert Laxalt," *REDEN (Revista Española de Estudios Norteamericanos)* 12 (1996), 128.
37 *Child of the Holy Ghost*, 152–153.
38 Robert Laxalt, *The Governor's Mansion* (Reno: University of Nevada Press, 1994), 3.
39 Laxalt, *The Governor's Mansion*, 3.
40 David Sibley, *Geographies of Exclusion: Society and Difference in the West* (New York: Routledge, 1995), 93.
41 Laxalt, *The Governor's Mansion*, 8–9.
42 Laxalt, *The Governor's Mansion*, 85.
43 Laxalt, *The Governor's Mansion*, 85.
44 Laxalt, *The Governor's Mansion*, 43.
45 Laxalt, *The Governor's Mansion*, 221.
46 Richard W. Etulain, "Robert Laxalt: Basque Writer of the American West," in *Portraits of Basques in the New World*, eds. Richard W. Etulain and Jeronima Echeverria (Reno: University of Nevada Press, 1999), 227.
47 Laxalt, *The Governor's Mansion*, 227. Italics in the original text.

The Influence of Robert Laxalt

Compiled by Gretchen Skivington,

Gretchen Skivington—Professor emerita of Humanities, Great Basin College

"Robert Laxalt legitimized the identity of American Basques in the 1960s–1980s—I should know, I was one of them! For us, his impact begins with the evocative *National Geographic* magazine articles and extends through his trilogy of novels. A scion of Nevada letters, he was "Frenchy" here in Elko where he once reluctantly served as MC at the National Basque Festival. My own American Basque novels, *Echevarria* and *Barria*, were greatly influenced by Laxalt. whom I met various times. We were coincidentally both working on Basque hotel novels in the mid-'80s: his, *The Basque Hotel,* mine, *Echevarria.* When I sheepishly asked him what advice he would give a young novelist, he, very Bob-like, graciously replied 'You do *you*, kid. Elko is my favorite town!'"

Beebs Turnbull—American Basque, genealogist, and writer

"My first recollection of Mr. Laxalt's work was reading a piece that Mr. Laxalt wrote for *National Geographic* magazine at my uncle's house when I was a teenager. I found a neat pile of the magazines on a table in my uncle's studio room. From the moment I recognized the subject material, I was quite intrigued to read on as I had never seen any articles about the Basque culture. At school, none of my friends had ever heard of a Basque person before I explained it. Most of the Basque stories I knew were from family stories or family traditions passed down from family members. From those conversations, I knew that Basque people traveled great lengths around the globe, to explore, and to work, and many like my family settled in America away from fear, persecution, and war. When I was reading Mr. Laxalt's words, I felt both cultural pride and a certain humbleness in that a Basque American writer could write so descriptively yet with such sensitivity, nobleness, and reverence to the Basque culture. As a wordsmith, Mr. Laxalt wrote so beautifully that I looked for more of his works to read, learn, and submerse myself in the Basque experience. To this day I encourage people, both Basques and non-Basques alike, to read Mr. Laxalt's works for his remarkable descriptions, literary timelessness, and the importance to the Basque diaspora. My mother was from Mundaka, and my grandfather was a Gudari. I am writing now about my mother and her family. She was part of the Silent Generation. I want to give her a voice."

Pete Ernaut—President, Government and Public Affairs at R&R Partners, native Nevadan

"Robert Laxalt's books meant a great deal to me. I believe I have read every one, some multiple times. *Sweet Promised Land*, in particular, was an outstanding book. Very moving from the very first, the epic line, 'My father was a sheepherder, and his home was the hills.' My grandfather was a sheepherder, and this story just as easily could have been a story about him or about thousands of other Basque immigrants who took the same path. It was insightful, inspiring, a profoundly well-written piece."

Anne M. Rogers—American Basque

"I met Robert and his brother at St. Étienne de Baïgorry about thirty years ago. We stayed at the same hotel, and I had a good talk with both. My mother came from the same town, and my dad was born and raised in St. Jean Pied de Port, the next village. My parents came to the US in 1917. We were raised in New Mexico. A very nice man."

Karmen Zaval Murphy—American Basque, Nevada native

"Robert Laxalt was the man he described as his father, Dominique—'luminous and tender.'"

Cyd McMullen—professor emerita of English, Great Basin College: Elko, Nevada

"As I reread some of Robert Laxalt's novels and essays, I am struck by the way he has captured Nevada small towns in the early twentieth century. Anyone who has lived in one during the 1950s–1960s as I have will recognize the atmosphere, the sense of place he has caught so well: the streets lined with poplars, cottonwoods, elms; the unpretentious houses populated by recognizable characters; children exploring their small worlds in freedom with little adult oversight. It is here in the hinterland, in the 'old heart of Nevada,' that Laxalt finds meaning. Human beings are shaped by the landscapes that they inhabit and the landscapes that they create around them. The towns are domesticated landscapes, human order in the shape of streets and houses and gardens scribed over wild land to hold back the harshness and extremes of the Great Basin. The mother in *The Basque Hotel* chooses to raise her children here, where the influences of school and church will fit them for easier lives. Her thickened legs mapped with purple veins testify to the costs of maintaining a home for children and boarders and an occasional haven for men who make their living outside the town limits in the deserts and mountains of Nevada.

Laxalt honors these men, 'men of leather and bronze, who had been rich as barons one day and broke and working for wages the next,' who 'even though they had battled with life, they had learned to accept it, because they had learned first to bow their heads to the winter blizzards and the desert sun.' His father, Dominique, in *Sweet Promised Land*, and the character of Pete's father in *The Basque Hotel* are men like these. The landscape of the Great Basin has honed boys, native born and newcomers alike, hungry for the opportunity to succeed into a particular kind of men, into Nevadans. Men who can live in the extremes of desert and mountain, in heat and snow, guarding thousands of sheep with only dogs for help and company, sleeping in bedrolls on the ground, matching wits with wily predators who kill for food or only to kill, living in isolation and loneliness fifty weeks a year. Lines from *Sweet Promised Land* describe the sacrifice of home and homeland, what the transformation from Basque immigrant to American has cost: 'I saw the West rising up at dawn with an awesome vastness of deserts and mighty mountain ranges. I saw a band of sheep wending their way down a lonely mountain ravine of sagebrush and pine, and I smelled their dust and heard their muted bleating and the lovely tinkle of their bells. I saw a man in crude garb with a walking stick following after with his dog, and once he paused to mark the way of the land. Then I saw a cragged face that the land had filled with hope and torn with pain, had changed from young to old, and in the end had claimed.' Laxalt's honest and loving portrayal of his family, his state, his home rings true to Nevadans who know his work and who honor him as a native son and the best writer our state has yet produced."

Jal Lounibos—California writer, historian

"When I was sixteen, my Basque father slipped *Sweet Promised Land* into my hands from his bookshelf, and he subsequently continued to share each of Robert Laxalt's books with me through the years. Papa loved him. Knew him personally. Loved speaking about him. Reading Laxalt transformed me—intimately introducing me to the Pyrenees and to the culture of the mountains as I had never known it then—four generations and almost one hundred years removed from our family's emigration. And it began a lifelong study of our roots and culture which continues today. In later years, several return trips to the 'Promised Land' allowed me to breathe in that rarified air and listen to the multiple languages and patois of my family villages, to feel what lay beneath the surface; to discover my fifth great-grandmother high in her frontier home of Urdos, and then to further that study through the research and study center Laxalt helped establish at the University of Nevada, Reno. Now I write my own stories and biographies of our ancestors so that our young generations may never lose touch with where we come from and how profound that influence still is upon us. Laxalt's influence? Stunning and profound. Has any one individual among our Basque people in America had a greater influence in sustaining our love and knowledge of our ancient culture? I doubt it—I have yet to meet such a soul—except perhaps my own beloved Papa."

Michael Fischer—retired Carson Valley dentist, Nevada historian

"As Basque by assimilation, I was educated by Robert Laxalt's writings about the Basques, their values, strengths, and indeed their weaknesses. I live around and work with Basque people, and his novels reinforced my daily encounters and experiences. Researching his family for history presentations, I learned that most of his writing was historically accurate with but just a little literary license. However, his greatest fit to me was describing the 'Old Nevada' that I experienced growing up! I have read most of his books multiple times and still enjoy them and always learn something new!"

Janet Pearce Petersen—Elko County historian, director of the Cowboy Arts & Gear Museum

"My mom went to college with Bob. He never forgot a name. Decades later, he'd see someone and have instant recall of who they were. I reread *Sweet Promised Land* and still love the simplicity of it. I remember reading *National Geographic* articles, amazed the Basque Country was just like the verbal descriptions I'd heard from immigrants from the old country. I was enchanted by the "old worldness" of it all. Many years later, I had the opportunity to visit the Basque Country. Things were quite a bit more modern by then, but still, it was like experiencing those wonderful photos and prose of Bob Laxalt's in the 1960s. It was magical!"

Denise Aguirre—student worker, Basque Studies Program, UNR, 1970s, and native Nevadan

"He was a great man. Laxalt and (William A.) Douglass—both great Nevadans."

Hank Nuwer—writer, editor of *The Fairbanks Daily News-Miner*

"My three-year paid assistantship at the University of Nevada ended, along with a monthly stipend. Those three years, I juggled teaching composition courses, my classwork, and freelance writing to pay the collective rent and grocery bills. The same time my university stipend ended, my wife and I agreed to divorce. Discouraged, perhaps depressed, I visited my mentor, Robert Laxalt, in his office at the University of Nevada Press. Laxalt, an author and instructor, wrote about Europe and South America for *National Geographic*. I was the grandson of a Polish orphan who farmed hogs, fowl, and dairy cattle. He was the son of French immigrant sheepherders. 'Bob' advised me without pay while I coedited the campus literary magazine for three years. I again asked his advice. 'You want to write, and you've come to hate graduate school?' he asked. He summed up in a sentence what it had taken me fifteen minutes to confess. 'Then I think you should quit the program and write full time,' Laxalt said. 'You've already published more than most professors in the English department.' 'What about teaching?' I asked him. 'Don't I need a doctorate?' 'Put together enough good publications, and some journalism program will hire you.' Which, precisely, had been Laxalt's own life's course from herder to writer to academic. With his blessing, that moment I wrote off three years of graduate school as an unredeemable disappointment and loss."

Willy Vlautin—musician, author of Nevada novels *The Motel Life*, *Northline,* and *Don't Skip Out on Me*

"Robert Laxalt was a huge influence from the moment I read *Sweet Promised Land* thirty years ago. His books have become my close friends. When I worked on *Don't Skip Out on Me*, I kept *Sweet Promised Land* and *The Basque Hotel* with me for a couple of years as saints to help the book. I'd always have them next to my computer so I could see them. Part of me always lives inside those books, inside that era and that time in Nevada. It's the place I go to when my own life falls apart or when I just need comfort."

Frank Bergon—author of *Shoshone Mike, Wild Game,* and *The Temptations of St. Ed and Brother S.*

"Bob's influence on me was primarily personal. I looked up to him as the country's most important Basque American writer, the one whose memoir generated Basque pride during the era of ethnic recognition, manifested in the first Basque festival he actively promoted in Sparks, and others in Elko and Los Banos that I attended with my relatives. I actually came to his books late because while I was struggling to write fiction, my first awareness of him was as a friend of my uncle Lou Mendive in Sparks, who knew Bob as a journalist and a writer of nonfiction, mainly his *National Geographic* articles and his memoir *Sweet Promised Land*. Before I knew of Bob's memoir, I published my first story at sixteen in my high school literary magazine about a Basque sheepherder named Fermin Erro. Bob hadn't yet written any fiction about Basques when I was publishing, other than early stories in college and as a Stegner Fellow, including a California ranch story, "Trippet's Dog," in an anthology reviewed in *The New York Times Book Review*. We came to know each other later through letters and phone calls and finally met after he published his first Nevada novel, *The Basque Hotel*, and I also published my first, *Shoshone Mike*. I describe a conversation with Bob in *The Toughest Kid We Knew* where we stretched out on his lawn after lunch. Again his influence was personal. He generously asked me to submit a novel to the University of Nevada Press that launched a fruitful relationship for me with the Press that he had the vision to found. He talked about my uncle, who as a football player and basketball star at the University of Nevada, and his own experience there as a boxer. That afternoon was also when he told me that as a kid he didn't know what the hell a Basque was. That revelation affected me deeply because, although we were of different generations, I shared his feeling. Like him, when young, I knew I was Basque but not what it meant historically or culturally. As I told Bob that day, what had opened my eyes were his *National Geographic* articles with photos in the late '60s and early '70s. Never before in the national press had I seen or read about Basques of my own experience. I also saw and learned for the first time something about the history of the country from which my grandparents came and where many of my relatives still lived. I clipped those pieces and cherished them for years. Looking back now, I realize that his admission that day helped me to go on to write about Basque American experience as I knew it. I didn't have to write about stereotypical immigrant Basque sheepherders. As in *Wild Game* and *Jesse's Ghost,* I could write about Basque American experience, especially of my generation both on ranches and in cities, even those of Basque heritage who didn't know what the hell a Basque was."

ROBERT LAXALT
WILDROSE
[illegible] BRYANT CANYON ROAD
CARSON CITY, NEVADA [illegible]

August 26, 1994 -

Dear Frank -

I just finished reading Shoshone Mike - and I am floored by it! Story - writing style - exhaustive research - all.

I had not wanted to read it before - for fear it would one day influence a novella that merits writing - when this ordeal of writing the third book of the family trilogy is done.

But Shoshone Mike episodes won't take me down any wrong paths. It is honest - and as far as I can see - accurate. I've had occasion to visit Surprise Valley this summer and talk to John Laxague + others, by way of another project.

You know - I first heard of the killings when I was a kid - from my father - who in 1911 was working at the Smoke Creek ranch. He mentioned casually that "Indiano was a relation of ours." No more - but it stuck in my mind when I later read about the episode.

My compliments on a book that will have a long life.

Robert Laxalt to Frank Bergon, August 26, 1994, Frank Bergon Literary and Pictorial Collection, Box 4, Folder 6: orange "Laxalt," Jon Bilbao Basque Library, University of Nevada, Reno.

Shaun Griffin—Nevada poet and activist

"For reasons I will not understand, Bob took me under his wing and over time I became very close to him and Joyce. I relied on him for the kind of counsel that comes from old souls—how do you navigate the world of literature—the tough parts—without so much as a hint of what needs to be done? Bob never wavered. He always told me, 'You're an artist, a poet. You already understand what you need to do.' Over time I learned to trust those words. Like he did for many others who started on this path, he believed in me before I did. I once asked him how he wrote *A Man in a Wheatfield*? It was such a seamless novel. He thought long, and said, 'I don't know—,' again, typical Bob—deferent, kind, unwilling to stake anything but the higher ground. Of course he knew how he did it—he trusted his voice and wrote through the doubt. I spent countless hours with him and Joyce in the last decade of his life in their Washoe Valley house, sometimes just doing nothing, being present while they talked or ate or cajoled each other as the long-married are wont to do. I felt, strangely and serenely, in the presence of family. Bob and Joyce were so good to me in those last years. They taught me how to care for other word workers as people—and really, when it's all said and done, that's what matters."

Naming the Angel

for Robert Laxalt, 1923-2001

Three days after your seventy-seventh spring
you left in silence, daffodils
bunched in those boxered hands,
the final book not yet opened,
the one we fought for these many springs,
waging our lives on a page,
what bloody fools we writers are,
naming this angel
that once, we hoped would last—

but you gave us other names:
Melville, Steinbeck, Shelley, and Crane—
and we broke our writerly oaths like bottles,
slapped those same Royal keys,
wrote those knuckles into the same moribund shelves
and when you shared the Plimpton interview,
we laughed at Hemingway's pompous self
but desperate to drink and fish with him,
waded in books, then memory as if we could—

and none of us held fire like you
who lives in the wheatfield, the promised land,
the shepherd's hotel, and I can't write a damn thing
that will save you from silence
on this, your seventy-seventh spring,
can't even wish you a daffodil
or the book we made together,
those words you spoke like a rosary
run down my face in salted water.

For six winters, I have read "To Build a Fire"
to my own sons, so vivid was your reading
of London's story, and when you handed us
the hundred book list, later the frayed cocktail
napkin with Walter Clark's favorites,
I knew there was no church for turning back Robert,
we had to write, even if it stripped flesh
like you are stripped now
and all will one day be—.

Anchored in this silence is an immigrant history
that will not shake one from its bough.
Already, you have begun to stretch another spring,
the carnal happiness given to what we lose, losing you.

Shaun Griffin, 2001

The (First) Western Basque Festival

by Monika Madinabeitia

Year 1959. "More than 5000 persons from twelve states gathered in the twin cities of Reno, Sparks, Nevada, on June 6–7 for the first Western Basque Festival," wrote Robert Laxalt for the festival tabloid.[1] He continues: "The celebration marked the first such major interstate gathering of Basques, their families, and friends from all parts of the West," which significantly marked Basques and forthcoming events within the Basque American community in the American West. The festival was considered extremely successful; "The organizing committee for the festival, made up of local Basques and their descendants, described the affair as 'a success beyond all our expectations.' "[2] This paper examines the creation of the First Western Basque Festival—initially termed the Western Basque Festival (WBF) by the organizers—its goals, accomplishments, and aftermath—by emphasizing Laxalt's involvement in it. The WBF has become a significant resource for exploring and understanding the rich traditions and history of the Basque people in the American West. From traditional music and dance to culinary delights and historical artifacts, this festival offered a captivating glimpse into the vibrant world of the Basques. The Jon Bilbao Basque Library's Western Basque Festival Collection[3] houses most of the documentation and literature that have been consulted for this purpose.

The Basque event sponsored by Nugget hotel-casino pioneer Dick Graves in 1959 marked the beginning of a cultural celebration that continues to this day. Inspired by his wife, Flora's,[4] Basque heritage and his own fascination with the Basque Country, Graves adorned one of the casino bars with intricate Basque motifs. His manager, John Ascuaga,[5] was also of Basque descent. Graves thought that holding a modest Basque festival would be financially profitable and thus broached his idea to two Basque Americans, namely Peter Echeverria,[6] attorney and state senator from Reno[7] and the highly acclaimed author and former United Press correspondent[8] Robert Laxalt. Both Echeverria and Laxalt were prominent figures in the Basque community of Reno and were crucial in the organization of the festival. It was highly important that the organizers have a good reputation. As we will discuss later, "[p]rior to 1959 . . . Basques of the American West were little noticed and consciously maintained a low group profile."[9] The status of the two main organizers ensured the prominence of the event, which many Basques attended. In other words, "[t]he prestige of the sponsor and the members of the organizing committee lent the festival an air of social and political importance, assuaging . . . the potential fears of some Basques that a public display of their ethnicity might provoke ridicule or even hostility."[10]

Echeverria and Laxalt were excited at the prospect. They believed that the festival would serve as a platform for Basques to showcase their ethnic cultural heritage and traditions, fostering a sense of unity and solidarity within the community. The organizers envisioned a celebration that would transcend mere entertainment, aiming to promote understanding and appreciation of Basque identity among both Basques and non-Basques alike. By highlighting the significance of their ethnicity in a public setting, Echeverria and Laxalt hoped to dispel any misconceptions or stereotypes surrounding the Basque people. They saw this as an opportunity to challenge preconceived notions and foster a greater sense of acceptance and respect for their community. The festival's success would not only validate the pride they felt in their heritage but also inspire future generations to embrace their Basque roots with confidence. As Echeverria later declared, "I felt it was time for we Basques to come out of the woodwork."[11]

Echeverria operated as the chairman and Laxalt as the secretary. They named an organizing committee that included both Old World and New World Basques. The combination of both sides was vital for the festival to be accepted by the Old World Basques, who often thought that American-born Basques were indifferent and thus had lost much of their heritage. Similarly, Echeverria and Laxalt bore in mind the different sides of the Basque Country when choosing Old World representatives. They hence included in the committee Basques from both sides of the Pyrenees, that is, from Iparralde[12] and Hegoalde:[13] Joe Micheo, [14] Martin Esain,[15] and Dominique (Domingo) Gascue.[16] The three highly respected Old World-born Basques were popular in their communities, either because they operated Basque hotels, they were active in the Basque culture of their area, or they were involved in Basque clubs. Thanks to the careful makeup of the committee, the festival was widely accepted and supported by the immigrant generation. In Laxalt's words, "We needed the Old World types if we were going to have credibility with the old timers."[17] By virtue of the popularity of the three Basque men, many locals volunteered to staff the events and activities that were being scheduled.[18]

Another obstacle to overcome was the choice of location for the event. Graves's casino was in Sparks, which fortunately confounded Old World regional distinctions. Sparks-Reno was conceived as a neutral geographical spot for one day for the community in California, consisting mainly of French and Nafarroan Basques, and Idaho, made up of Bizkaians. Back then, the Reno-Sparks area was the only Basque colony in the United States with large numbers of French and Spanish Basques. Therefore, the Reno-Sparks location constituted a geographical and ethnic crossroad for the American West Basques.[19]

As for the committee, to make sure that it also contemplated the whole Basque American West of the time, in addition to Robert Laxalt and Peter Echeverria, it contained other four Basque Americans: John Laxalt,[20] Paul Parraguirre,[21] Peter Supera,[22] and the already mentioned Ascuaga.[23] Thanks to the extensive ties and places of residence of all members, they were able to reach a large contingent of Basques in Nevada. However, since it was decided to give the festival a wider regional significance, the committee had to make use of their ties and other personal qualities to encompass the whole West. The Basque population was scattered all through the extensive West, with no formal infrastructure or information network among them. Additionally, Basques remained reticent about publicly showing their ethnicity even though they were no longer viewed negatively as in the early days, which increased the challenge for the festival committee to reach them and tout the event.

Before 1959, several communities had their own annual picnic, considered the precursor to the WBF. They were exclusive to the Basque community, serving as a way for them to maintain their cultural traditions and connect with their fellow Basques. However, as the Basque population began to assimilate into American society, there was a shift in the purpose and organization of these events. The WBF aimed to bring together not only Basques but also people from diverse backgrounds who were interested in experiencing and learning about Basque culture. The 1959 festival "was the first one in history in the American West to display Basqueness publicly. And it appeared to be the catalyst for the same type of festivals to take place in more and more Basque local communities." By highlighting traditional music, sports, dance performances, authentic cuisine, and alike, they aimed to create an immersive Basque experience that included both Old World and New World elements. This inclusivity and public manifestation meant a significant departure from the previous private picnics and required a different approach from the festival committee. They had to find innovative ways to promote the event and attract attendees from various settings. This involved reaching out to local media outlets and collaborating with other community members to spread awareness about the festival. The committee recognized that showcasing the Basque heritage would be key to enticing people of different backgrounds to attend.

The context of the civil rights movement that started in the 1950s brought a sense of ethnic pride to ethnic groups, Basque Americans included. Besides, after the 1940s, the legislation started to favor the entry of Basque shepherds because they had been esteemed as a necessary part of the ranching labor force.[24] The participation of Basques in World War II also blessed the Basque community; hundreds of Basque Americans joined the US Army and were highly motivated to fight for their host country.[25] Laxalt himself interrupted his studies to enlist in the army.[26] All in all, the service given by Basque Americans in World War II helped them be acknowledged as good American citizens, which smoothed their assimilation process into the mainstream to some extent. In addition, another modifier of the image of the Basques was the postwar admiration of urban Americans for romanticizing the rural. This idealization of the Basque shepherds further enhanced their image and added to their mystique. The rugged rural landscapes became synonymous with adventure and freedom in the eyes of urban Americans. The shepherds were seen as guardians of tradition, preserving a way of life that was untouched by modernity. Their simplicity and solitude were romanticized, making them symbols of authenticity in a rapidly changing world. This romanticized image not only elevated the status of Basque Americans but also fueled a fascination with their culture and heritage.

Henceforth, in the second half of the twentieth century, the image of the Basque shepherd increasingly gained popularity. This stage may be considered the beginning of the process of invention (versus reinvention or resurgence) since it was a new emerging phenomenon within the Basque ethnic community.[27] Until then, before the 1950s, Basque ethnic identity was in many cases dormant, although many lived Basque on a regular basis. It was "more a fact of life, a lived reality, than a project."[28] In the Basque experience, it was expressed by the creation of Basque formal clubs, which in some cases even culminated in the building of Basque houses. The earliest Basque associations in the United States were created to respond to specific needs, such as helping their members in emergency medical situations, operating as insurance agencies, and providing social security, death benefits, or repatriation. The associations whose primary goals were to gather Basques on special occasions, such as balls or picnics, came later. Within the context of the roots phenomenon and the urge to be ethnic, "ethnic identity maintenance became a salvage operation, something that had to be worked out, a project rather than a lived daily reality."[29] Almost all the institutions were formed after the 1959 festival, which became a determinant instrument within the Basque experience in the American West.

All members of the committee were key to the flourishing completion of the festival, but as noted, Echeverria and Robert Laxalt were the prime movers. Aside from their personal skills and ties, their professional profiles became vital for the festival. For example, Echeverria, a state senator in the Nevada Legislature and one of Nevada's most prominent trial lawyers, was a loquacious orator. That proved to be an extremely useful skill when he and Laxalt visited the Basque Center in Boise, Idaho, and several Basque picnics in California to promote the festival.[30] Similarly, Laxalt's incredibly successful publication of *Sweet Promised Land* in 1957, which received national recognition, paved the way for the 1959 phenomenon. Through the story of his father, Dominique, Laxalt gave the Basques a creation story, a narrative to which they could relate. Dominique's particular story as an immigrant in the American West and that of Laxalt as the child of immigrant parents resonated with the individual stories of almost all Basques in the West. In doing so, Dominique and Laxalt's story became universal in the Basque community and, to some degree, in other immigrant groups. That is to say, the bond between the particular and the collective meaningfully started thanks to *Sweet Promised Land*. We may hence consider that Laxalt himself became a model to a certain extent for many Basques in the West. Laxalt's success story inspired and motivated others in the Basque community to strive for similar achievements. His personal journey also highlighted the importance of education and hard work in attaining one's goals. His parents' determination and resilience served as a shining example for future generations, proving that with dedication and perseverance, anything is possible. Furthermore, Laxalt's siblings' diverse career paths showcased the multitude of opportunities available in America. Whether pursuing politics, law, or religious vocations, they demonstrated that individuals could carve their own unique paths to success. Laxalt's story became a symbol of hope and possibility for individuals from different backgrounds who sought to achieve their own American Dream. Laxalt's book and life achievements stand as timeless tributes to the immigrant experience and powerful testaments to the enduring power of the American Dream. Consequently, Laxalt's involvement in the preparation of the festival and the creation story that emerged from it showcased his unique ability to capture the essence of the immigrant experience.

As will be argued later, because of Laxalt's literary gift, he grew into the main chronicler and narrator of the festival. One of the aims of his accounts was to promote the event to its fullest. He traveled out of state to publicize the festival, along with Echeverria, at a time when both had a regional reputation. Furthermore, the festival's association with a renowned casino added credibility. Graves's casino spared no expense, investing in brochures, photography, and advertising. Additionally, Graves generously funded the travel expenses of Echeverria and Laxalt, going as far as arranging chartered aircraft for their transportation. This comprehensive approach not only expedited the festival's success but also contributed to the creation of a narrative that embodied four Ps: prestige, prosperity, prowess, and pride. The combined efforts of all these elements culminated in an event that surpassed expectations and left a lasting impression on all who attended.

One other hardship to overcome was the inexperience of the committee in organizing festivals and their ignorance about the customs in the Basque Country. In Laxalt's case, that knowledge expanded later, during his two-year stay and further visits to the Basque Country. However, they had to rapidly learn about the old ways since the preparations started only a few months before the festival took place. The organizers felt forced to be creative to come up with solutions in a short amount of time. For example, since there was not a generic festival in the Basque Country from which they could learn, their starting point was the annual picnics or barbecues held locally in the West. As said, because of the magnitude and range of the event, the commission had to first explore their own culture before being able to sketch a program that would satisfy both the Old and New World Basques.

Becoming acquainted and familiar with Basque customs was crucial for the festival to respond to the needs and interests of both the Old and New Worlds. It was highly important that the first generation find features of the home they had left behind. Consequently, it was decided that "[f]estivities will be patterned after old-country feast day celebrations in the Pyrenees mountains between France and Spain, where the Basque kingdom held sway until its conquest and division."[31] In similar fashion, several of the drafts typed by Laxalt indicate his intention to highlight the traditional nature of the events scheduled for the festival, an intention that had at least a two-fold objective: that the events would be approved by the Old West Basques and that the New World Basques would learn about the traditions of the Basque Country. Therein, one of his drafts explains that "[a]ttired in colorful old-country costumes, the Idaho dancers will . . . portray the original dances of the ancient Basque kingdom between France and Spain." Then he explained further: "Included in the Idaho dancing program will be . . . the *Aurresku*, a fast-moving dance . . . and several variations of *La Jota*, traditional dance of the Basque [C]ountry."[32] Another draft gathers the name of the dance in Basque and a little explanation about it in English, for example, the "'Godalet Danza,' the wine glass dance; 'Sagar Dantza,' the apple dance; and 'Makil Dantza,' the dance of the sticks."[33] Since, as noted, the event had to similarly house New World components, it also contained a sheep camp exhibit and served the food of Basque hotels. It also held a barbecue, where loaves of shepherd's bread and the Basque American drink *picon* punch were sold.[34]

Non-Basques had to also be instructed about the Basque community, its history, and customs, for they were also welcome at the festival. Laxalt writes that "[a]lthough the Festival is limited to Basque, their families, and friends, a limited number of the general public will be admitted on the Festival day with an additional premium of the purchase of a Basque beret for men and a neckerchief for women."[35] As explained, this was not the first festival held in the American West, but it was the first to be public. In fact, one of its aims, although initially subtle, was to showcase the good nature of Basques. That meant that the public had to also be mentored before and after the festival, for which activities were included. Although it did not ultimately take place, there was a *bota* contest arranged for the non-Basques. In one of Laxalt's documents addressed to Don Jones, "For *Sports Illustrated* photograph,"[36] Laxalt clarified that "[t]he *bota* is a traditional Basque wineskin. I believe the true Basque word for it is *chahakoa*. . . . It is made of goatskin turned inside out, with the hair remaining inside . . . Surprisingly, this combination gives the wine no taste but its own."[37] He then explained how it "is gripped at the neck with the right hand and squeezed at the base with the left hand. This shoots a jet of wine into the mouth and down the throat. The lips never touch the opening to the wineskin."[38] Laxalt accounted for its tradition and use in almost all sheep camps in the West and still at the time, "partly from habit and partly because of the practical reasons of easy carrying."[39] Laxalt added a comment about how wine smugglers across the Pyrenees between France and Spain found it easier to carry huge wineskins than barrels of wine.[40] Interestingly, Laxalt included a bracketed observation on wine smuggling, describing it as "a Basque passtime."[41] It's likely "passtime" is a typo, and that he meant "pastime." Laxalt may have wanted to provide the audience with a much simpler definition and decriminalize the activity before the American public. He seems to make it sound like a common thing among Basques, almost like a tradition. Back then, under Francisco Franco's dictatorship, poor families supplemented their income by smuggling coffee, tobacco, and livestock. Within the Basque population, it was rarely considered an illicit activity but rather a means to battle the tough conditions through which many families had to live. Many sacrificed themselves so they could feed their families. All in all, Laxalt's goal was to educate and engage the community at large to foster a deeper understanding and appreciation for Basque culture. These efforts not only ensured the success of the festival but also created a lasting impact on the wider community and made the festival more than just a celebration.

Once it was decided that the festival would have a wider regional significance, the aim of the organizing committee was to attract as many Basques as possible to Reno. Laxalt, as noted, was a seasoned journalist, a writer, and an accomplished publicist. His previous work as a correspondent for the United Press provided him with the skills to write feature stories. He issued weekly news releases as the festival took shape. The stories were written from a human-interest perspective. Several were chosen by the wire services and ultimately appeared in the *San Francisco Chronicle* and *The New York Times*. These writings were so successful that even the *Voice of America* planned to broadcast news of the festival to Europe, both in Spanish and French.[42] Laxalt also reached out to the *Nevada State Journal, Reno Evening Gazette, United Press International, Associated Press, Time, Las Vegas Review-Journal, Sunset Magazine, San Francisco News,* and the *Territorial Enterprise*, among others. George Rosse, from the *Oakland Tribune*, told Laxalt that if he got to publish the news in *The Sacramento Bee, Stockton Record, Modesto Bee, Fresno Bee, Chronicle, and the Oakland Tribune*, then the news would be spread throughout Northern California.[43] The news must have made it, for in Mrs. Anne Aguilar Santuca's (Sacramento) letter to Laxalt, she indicated that she had read about "the Spanish Basque Celebration"[44] in *The Sacramento Bee*.[45] Others, such as Mrs. J. P. Elissondo (Walnut Creek, California), contacted Laxalt to let him know that they were unable to make it that time but that they hoped to see them at the next one.[46] In a letter addressed to Mrs. Guccini, Loma (Colorado), dated May 13, Laxalt appreciated her reading his book *Sweet Promised Land* and announced that he should have another one coming in a few months, also about the Basque people. Laxalt expressed that the festival "is really going to be an affair" and confessed that if they "live through it, [he] personally [is] going to run back to the hills for some peace." Laxalt, compared to other letters, greets Mrs. Guccini goodbye in Basque by adding "Ikous arte" before signing off.[47] Although Laxalt could no longer speak Basque, which was his mother tongue until he and his family moved to Carson City, Nevada, he could still understand it.[48]

The organization and accomplishments of the WBF increased Laxalt's attachment to the Basque world. The initial discovery of the Old World and its peoples through his first visit with his father, Dominique, later articulated in words, was boosted by the findings he came across while organizing the festival. In his letter to Mrs. Guccini, Laxalt admitted that they were not conscious of what they had started or how many Basques there were in the West, but that they were "sure finding out."[49] The high number of Basques struck him as positive. We may presume that Laxalt's awareness of Basques in the Far West was initiated after the success of his book and through the many letters he received to congratulate him on *Sweet Promised Land.* However, bearing in mind his comment to Mrs. Guccini, one must wonder whether Laxalt was genuinely cognizant of how large the Basque community really was until he started with the big event. It would be safe to suspect that Laxalt himself found his engagement in the preparation of the festival a motivational driver and a means to construct his identities, ethnic and civic, before the actual event took place. Thus, by June 6–7, 1959, Laxalt himself had experienced some degree of fluidity between different identities, which he exchanged and nurtured with the other committee members and likewise transmitted both consciously and unconsciously through the festival. Probably still unaware of it, Laxalt was involved in providing "a communicative scenery for manifestations of ethnicity and cultural unity,"[50] a stimulating and effective platform to develop Basque ethnic identity and contribute to the social cohesion of the community. The positive emotional self-regard that Laxalt must have undergone during his active involvement very likely impacted the larger Basque collective favorably. This process was probably one of the keys to generating the communal bond that emanated from the WBF, which played a central role in fostering emotional attachment to the Basque identity. It created a system of reciprocity and shared responsibility and experience. Bearing in mind that Basques were only beginning to be visible within mainstream America, psychologically motivating drivers had to be created and promoted.

It is within this context of psychological motivation and affective attachment that Laxalt's networking ability created a communal domino effect. In other words, the shared connection that was emerging accelerated the urge for collaboration and participation in a collective effort. For instance, Espe Alegria[51] hosted a radio program, *The Basque Program*, known as the "Voice of the Basques," from 1955 to 1981. The broadcast was in Basque, and countless shepherds in the area listened to it,[52] making Alegria a crucial part of the "word by mouth" means to let Basques in Boise know about the festival in Reno. As a result of this domino effect, Laxalt was also able to ask Alegria about other Basques. In a letter dated May 19, 1959, Alegria refers to a phone call received by Laxalt and tells him that she has spoken to Teles Hormaechea,[53] as she had promised. The topic is the distribution of prizes for the different variants of weightlifters, which are specified in the letter. Alegria claims that the festival has caused "quite a lot of enthusiasm," that "there will be quite a few people going from" Boise. and that she herself is looking forward to it.[54] Within this causal sequence, affiliated organizations of

Wool Growers, Sheep Growers, and Sheep and Goat Raisers' Associations were also sent information about the festival so that they could reach out to the Basque community. Laxalt wrote letters to the respective secretaries to spread the word about the festival. In one such letter, dated April 15, 1959, sent to Mr. H. B. Embach, the secretary of the Arizona Wool Growers Association (Phoenix), Laxalt tells him about the festival and how they "hope to have several thousand Basques, their families, and friends on hand for the event."[55] Laxalt continues to write that they, the organizers, have "prepared display posters about the Festival for distribution to Basque hotels and bars throughout the West" and that he would like to ask Embach "to send [them] the addresses of these establishments and gathering places in [Embach's] area or state" because, on behalf of the committee, they believe "that posters and news releases will be the main way in which [they] hope to contact [their] people." Laxalt finishes the letter hoping that Embach will be able to attend, and reminds him that "the invitation goes to any sheepmen or cattlemen [he] may know."[56] In a reply to Laxalt, dated April 28, 1959, M. C. Claar, secretary of the Idaho Wool Growers Association in Boise, declares that he is "very pleased to enclose a list of Basque houses in Idaho,"[57] which was supplied by Benito Ysursa, the owner and manager of the Valencia Club in Boise. Claar laments not being able to attend the festival, but explains that in their organization they "have considerable work with Basque people and that they make up the greater part of the work force on behalf of sheep owners."[58] Claar then adds that they "carried a brief announcement of this festival in an issue of the Wool Growers Bulletin," which was sent to all sheepmen in Idaho and that they "acknowledge receipt of applications for tickets and the poster which [they] will keep in [their] office."[59] One must admit that at a time when there was no internet or mobile phones, the committee used all means possible and was successful in spreading the word about the festival by creating a network as a result of the aforementioned domino effect. As already indicated, Laxalt was undoubtedly a key figure in the communication department. In addition to his arduous effort to promote the festival, Laxalt also reached out to get Basque motifs with the aim of creating a Basque ambience at the festival. For example, he contacted France's tourist office in San Francisco, to get such material. He was sent a twenty-five-pound package with descriptive literature on the Basque country and the Pyrenees; one hundred small cardboard pieces to decorate dining tables; 120 blue, white, and red balloons, and thirty posters of the Pyrenees region.[60]

Although tickets did not have to be bought in advance, "the Western Basque Festival urge[d] that Basques, their families, and friends make early applications so that they may know how many to prepare for." To do so, Laxalt gave his own home address in Reno; hence the huge number of letters that were addressed to him, often under the title Western Basque Festival. However, Laxalt must have been used to getting abundant correspondence, for, as noted, he had received hundreds of letters of appreciation from Basques from all over the West after his success with *Sweet Promised Land.* In fact, his file of return addresses became the core of the mailing list for the announcement of the festival.[61] This list was the starting point for special invitations to ambassadors, consulates, Nevada authorities, and so on.[62] Again, Laxalt's book had not only laid the foundations for a receptive community on both sides of the Atlantic but had also turned out to be highly useful for the promotion of the festival.

This festival may not have been the first in the American West, but as previously indicated, it was the first to openly manifest Basqueness. Not only that, the 1959 festival also served as a pattern for the many other celebrations and festivals that came afterward: "Today's festivals all date from the original 1959 event and are almost carbon copies of it."[63] For example, the festival included an exhibit about Basque herding in the West. Nowadays, sheep wagons, tents, or sheep camp outfits are still displayed. Such items may be perceived as elements of the past in contemporary events, but back in 1959 they were still part of the recent history of Basques in America. As Laxalt was getting out his father's old sheep camp outfit to set up on the festival grounds, Dominique's old dog, Barbo, saw "the old outfit being unlimbered and though crippled and lame with arthritis he had yelped and cavorted at the prospect of going back to the hills where he belongs." Sadly for Barbo, "the camp was only going to a parking lot. And Barbo's master Dominique, . . . in his early seventies and stooped with arthritis of his own in spite of his lean, tanned, high-cheeked face, the still-keen eye and voice—Dominique said . . . for both of them . . . : 'I can't go to the sheep camp any more.' "[64] This little story of Dominique represents the big picture of what was happening at the time. The solitary shepherds who had endured the harshness of the West were aging and becoming part of a bygone era. The shepherds' traditional way of life was fading away, as the younger generation sought education and urban opportunities. The hills that had been their home for generations now seemed like a distant memory, as progress and modernity took over. The once revered shepherds, known for their resilience and connection to nature, were now left with only remnants of their herding gear and a sense of nostalgia. The solitude they had cherished was replaced by the bustling noise of cities. As they looked back at their past, they could not help but feel a mixture of pride for preserving a dying tradition and sadness for the loss of a way of life that had defined them for so long. The year 1959 meant a farewell to the disappearing Basque West and a welcome to the new Basque America that was emerging.

The festival was an interplay of tradition and innovation, and Basques in the West did not want to miss this change of era: "As they never had before, such men came to Reno and Sparks, this past weekend, with their women and sons and daughters. They came from twelve states . . . People with names like Echeverria, Yparraguirre, Goitiandia, Urresti and Etchemendy. And when they were gathered there were more than 5,000 of them.[65] The festivities began on a Saturday evening with a testimonial dinner for visiting dignitaries, followed by a public dance featuring the music of Jim Jausoro, from Boise. On Sunday morning, a Catholic mass was celebrated before an overflow crowd in Reno's St. Thomas Aquinas Cathedral. This was followed by a graveside memorial service for US Senator Patrick A. McCarran of Nevada, "the Basques' political patron saint."[66] Next there was a sheepdog exhibition, a tournament for players of the Basque card game called *mus*, and folkdance performances by dancers from Reno, Boise, and San Francisco. A choral group from Winnemucca presented Basque songs, as did a professional Basque *txistulari*, or flute and drum player, from New York City. The musical selections were representative of the Old World regional music traditions. There were athletic contests, including weightlifting, woodchopping, and a tug-of-war between sheepmen and cattlemen. A sheep camp was set up as a display for those who were curious about the herder's lifestyle. In the late afternoon, there was an enormous barbecue featuring the fare common to the Basque hotels of the American West. The festival concluded on Sunday evening with another public dance.[67]

The festival may have concluded on June 7, 1959, but its effect had just started. After 1959, different Basque communities in the American West started progressively coming together around formal institutions through which they displayed Old and New World legacies. Elko's first National Basque Festival in 1964 deserves special attention. Basque people in Elko have had their private annual picnic since the 1940s, but after the creation of the club in 1959, they opened their picnic to the public. After 1964, it grew: Elko's picnic became one of the biggest in the area, attracting people from other areas and forging the imagery that the First Western Basque Festival had set up: the display of both Basque and American identities. In 1964, the First National Basque Festival was held on the Fourth of July, the United States Day of Independence. The year was also important as it commemorated the centennial of the State of Nevada. In doing so, Basques emphasized their attachment and contribution to the building of Nevada and, therefore, the United States. [68] This devotion to Nevada and America is also clearly manifested in Laxalt's works, including *The Violent Land: Tales the Old Timers Tell* (1953), *Nevada* (1970), *Nevada: A Bicentennial History* (1977), and *A Lean Year and Other Stories* (1994).

On June 11, 1959, Mary Spring wrote a letter to Laxalt. Spring starts the letter by claiming that she was one of the five folk dancers from Fresno, California, who attended the Basque festival and that "it will always remain an unforgettable experience . . . Already they are looking forward to the next one!"[69] Her second paragraph emotively expresses that she was "very happy to be able to report to [her] mother that the Basques 'of other times' . . . are still with [them]. For a long time [her mother] has been saying that the Basques here in America are so different from those in the Pyrenees"[70] and that "[t]he Basque language is dying out, they are tearing down all the old Basque hotels in San Francisco, no one does any of the old dances or sings the old songs, and they have forgotten their religion and their heritage."[71] Spring cheerfully states that at the festival she heard Basque language all around her, "spoken by the young folks as well as the older folks."[72] She then apologizes for not being able to speak it since her father was French and they spoke Spanish at home. According to Spring, "the church was packed with Basques on Sunday morning; the old dances and songs were there."[73] She adds another paragraph indicating that "[a]s a Basque, and for [her] husband and [her] friends who were there—whose parents . . . although non-Basque come from foreign countries—they want to thank [Laxalt] and the members of the committee most sincerely for promoting the perpetuation of Basque folklore in this country in such a wonderful way."[74] On the second page of her letter, when nearly running out of space, Spring writes, "If I sound proud of my Basque heritage, I am."[75] And then finishes by adding, in Basque, "Zure osagarriari!"[76]

On balance, the festival was highly successful. The Western Basque Festival—baptized as the First Western Basque Festival afterward—enabled Basques in the American West to publicly display their ethnicity. The strong anti-Basque bias and newspapers of the early twentieth century, as is evident in "they [Bascos] have some undesirable characteristics that the Chinese are free from. They [Bascos] are filthy, treacherous . . . meddlesome [and] undesirable . . ."[77] were substituted, as reflected in the *Nevada State Journal* in 1959,[78] by words of praise and admiration. Basques were described as "industrious characters," with a "tremendous reputation for honesty," indicating that "[t]he old phrase 'his word is as good as his bond' could not be applied more aptly than to the Basques." The dignitaries who attended the festival, which included American, Spanish, French, and Basque eminences, were the effect of the prestige that the committee and the sponsor had. Additionally, the presence of authorities increased the status of the event, which certainly favored the image of the Basques.

The festival provided the chance for a story that the Basques could tell about themselves. In addition, it allowed Basques to come to terms with who they were, as many, Laxalt included, did not know what it meant to be Basque. They were able to witness that they were not alone and that they could safely claim that they were both American and Basque. The festival triggered a sense of collectiveness and community, as well as a visceral and emotional bond with Basqueness and the people. This emotional attachment affected individuals and the collective in terms of identity. By 1959, they had assimilated into the mainstream, but they had not forgotten where they and their people came from. The First Western Basque Festival played a central role in raising self-awareness and building solid and enduring connections. The festival served as a platform for Basque Americans to proudly display their unique traditions and customs, fostering a sense of belonging and pride within the community. The event also provided an opportunity for younger generations to learn about their roots and understand the sacrifices made by their ancestors. Moreover, the festival acted as a catalyst for intergenerational connections, bringing together elders who had preserved their heritage with younger individuals eager to embrace it. This interplay between past and present created a powerful sense of continuity and unity among Basque Americans in the West.

Today, as we reflect on the First Western Basque Festival, we recognize its lasting impact on shaping the Basque American identity in the region. The festival left an indelible mark on Basque American identity, shaping it in ways that continue to resonate. It stands as a testament to the enduring legacy of Basque culture and its profound impact on the fabric of American society in the West. The festival served as a vibrant celebration of Basque culture and an opportunity for both Basque Americans and the wider community to come together in appreciation of Basque heritage and identity. Laxalt's involvement also stands as a testimony in the Basque American society of the West. Through his collaboration, Laxalt not only preserved and promoted Basque heritage, but also influenced the larger narrative of American history by showcasing the contributions of the Basque community in shaping the nation's identity.

Works Cited

1999 Renoko Aste Nagusia (booklet). 1999.

Camus, Argitxu. *The North American Basque Organizations (NABO), Incorporated: Ipar Amerikako Euskal Elkarteak 1973–2007.* Gasteiz: Central Publications Service of the Basque Government, 2002.

"Descendants of the Pyrenees Gather Here for Festival," *Nevada State Journal* (Reno), June 4, 1959.

Douglass, William A. "Inventing an Ethnic Identity: The First Basque Festival," in *Global Vasconia,* 132–144. Reno: Center for Basque Studies, 2006.

____. "Interstitial Culture, Virtual Ethnicity, and Hyphenated Basque Identity in the New Millennium," in *Nevada Historical Quarterly*, 43–2, (2000), 155–165.

____. "Basque American Identity: Past Perspectives and Future Projects," in *Changing in the American West, Exploring the Human Dimension,* edited by Stephen Tchudi, 183–199. Reno and Las Vegas: Nevada Humanities Committee and University of Nevada Press, 1996.

Elustondo, Miel. *Western Basque Festival 1959: Urte Hartan Gertatu Zen.* Zarautz: Susa, 2007.

Kuutma, Kristin. "Festival as Communicative Performance and Celebration of Ethnicity," *Folklore* 7 (1998): 1–5. 10.7592/FEJF1998.07.festiva.

Laxalt, Robert. *The Violent Land: Tales the Old Timers Tell.* Reno: University of Nevada Press, 1953.

____. *Sweet Promised Land.* Reno: University of Nevada Press. 1957.

____. *Nevada.* Reno: University of Nevada Press, 1971.

____. *Nevada: A Bicentennial History*. Reno: University of Nevada Press,1977.

____. *A Lean Year and Other Stories*. Reno. University of Nevada Press, 1994.

Passehl, Erin. "Espe Alegria: Cultural Advisor and Voice of the Basques in American Radio." Presentation, Boise, Idaho, July 30, 2010.

"Sheepmen and Biscayans," *Caldwell Tribune* (Idaho), July 17, 1909.

Western Basque Festival Collection, BAQ103. Jon Bilbao Basque Library, University Libraries, University of Nevada, Reno. https://archive.library.unr.edu/public/repositories/4/resources/3983. Accessed June 21, 2023.

Notes

1 “Copy for Festival Tabloid,” Western Basque Festival Collection.

2 “Copy for Festival Tabloid,” Western Basque Festival Collection.

3 Summarized and referred to as WBFC in this paper when giving credit to the documentation archived by the Jon Bilbao Library at the Center for Basque Studies (University of Nevada, Reno.) Since the material is not archived under specific titles or topics, usually WBFC is the only reference given in the article. Other times, the author has added generic titles, although these do not comply with the archive's filing/naming system. When the documents have titles, these have been used as reference.

4 Dick and Flora were both Boise, Idaho, natives. Flora was born to Spanish Basque immigrants and introduced Dick to the Basque culture. The original Nugget in Sparks opened in 1955. (“1999 Renoko Aste Nagusia” booklet).

5 Born to Basque parents, Ascuaga began working with Dick Graves in Idaho as a food manager and moved with him to Nevada. Together with his wife, Rose, whose family was from the French side of the Basque Country, they built John Ascuaga's Nugget Hotel/Casino into the major resort destination in the Reno area. (“1999 Renoko”).

6 Born in 1918, in Idaho to Basque parents, Echeverria was admitted to the Nevada State Bar in 1949 and practiced law in Reno until 1983. He then operated a consulting firm specializing in gaming, real estate, and legal matters. Echeverria was elected to the Nevada State Senate from Washoe County, 1959 to 1963. (“1999 Renoko”).

7 “A little-known people,” WBFC.

8 “A little-known people,” WBFC.

9 William A. Douglass, “Inventing an Ethnic Identity,” in *Global Vasconia* (Reno: Center for Basque Studies 2006), 133.

10 Douglass, "Inventing," 141.

11 Douglass, "Inventing," 138.

12 French Basque Country.

13 Spanish Basque Country.

14 Born in the Spanish side of the Basque Country in 1891, Micheo immigrated to the US in 1908. He moved to Gardnerville in 1937, where he ran the French Hotel. Later he opened the Pyrenees hotel. He died In 1968. ("1999 Renoko").

15 Born in 1905 in Aldude (France), Esain came to the United States in 1927 to work as a sheepherder in Elko, Nevada. In 1942, he started bartending for Louise Etcheverry at the Santa Fe Hotel in Reno, and they became partners in 1944. In 1949, Martin opened the new Santa Fe Hotel. Martin died in 1966. ("1999 Renoko").

16 From Banka, in the French Pyrenees, Gascue herded sheep and worked and ran several Basque hotels. In the 1950s, Dominique served as president of the Basque American Club in Reno. ("1999 Renoko").

17 Douglass, "Inventing," 140.

18 Douglass, "Inventing," 140.

19 Douglass, "Inventing," 138.

20 Robert Laxalt's brother, John Laxalt practiced law until 1971 and was a legislative/business consultant in Washington, DC He died in 2011. ("1999 Renoko").

21 Born in 1989 in San Francisco, Parraguirre managed the Parraguirre family sheep ranch in Nevada until 1920. He became associated with the Union Oil Company and then worked for the Mono County Assessor's office for sixteen years. He died in 1980. ("1999 Renoko").

22 Born in 1921 in Carson City, Supera worked for the State of Nevada and was elected Justice of the Peace in Carson City. He was later elected recorder/auditor and retired in 1985. He died in 1997. ("1999 Renoko").

23 WBFC.

24 Douglass, "Inventing," 137.

25 See "Fighting Basques" (https://www.fightingbasques.net/en-us/Fighting-Basques).

26 See Laxalt's *A Private War: An American Code Officer in the Belgian Congo* (1998).
27 William A. Douglass, "Basque American Identity: Past Perspectives and Future Projects," in *Changing in the American West, Exploring the Human Dimension,* ed. Stephen Tchudi (Reno and Las Vegas: Nevada Humanities Committee and University of Nevada Press, 1996), 191.
28 Douglass, William A. "Interstitial Culture, Virtual Ethnicity, and Hyphenated Basque Identity in the New Millennium," in *Nevada Historical Quarterly*, 43-2, (2000), 156.
29 Douglass, "Interstitial," 156
30 Douglass, "Inventing," 140.
31 Western Basque Festival, Zazpiak-Bat, "about the festival," WBFC.
32 Press, WBFC.
33 Press, WBFC.
34 Rinehart "the old people," 6-7, WBFC.
35 Press, WBFC.
36 WBFC.
37 Press, WBFC.
38 Press, WBFC.
39 Press, WBFC.
40 His remark on smuggling hints his latent interest in Basque topics and customs. He developed the topic on smuggling in the early 1970s and as an outcome, in 1985 he published the short novel *A Cup of Tea in Pamplona,* which was the first to be set in the Basque Country. It was nominated for a Pulitzer Prize and one of his few works translated into Basque, *Kafea Hartzen Iruñean*, in 1986.
41 Press, WBFC.
42 Douglass, "Inventing," 141.
43 Elustondo, Miel, *Western Basque Festival 1959: Urte Hartan Gertatu Zen* (Zarautza: Susa, 2007), 28.
44 As referred to by Mrs. Anne Aguilar in her letter. Correspondence. WBFC.
45 WBFC.
46 WBFC.

47 WBFC.

48 Linguistic observation by Castor de Uriarte (Euskaltzaindi[a]) in his letter to Sr. D. Ignacio Mª de Echaide, Presidente de la Academia de la Lengua Vasca, July 27,1959, WBFC.

49 WBFC.

50 Kuutma, Kristin, "Festival as Communicative Performance and Celebration of Ethnicity," *Folklore* 7 (1998), 1.

51 Alegria (1906-1991) was a Boise resident who was born in the Basque Country and spent her life preserving and promoting Basque language and culture in Boise. "Espe Alegria's continuous work left a legacy on the American Diaspora in three areas: her work in radio broadcasting, translation and immigration services, and the arts. Espe hosted *The Basque Program*, a one-hour radio program that aired every week from 1955–1981" (Passehl, Erin, "Espe Alegria: Cultural Advisor and Voice of the Basques in American Radio." Presentation, Boise, July 30, 2010).

52 Passehl, "Espe Alegria."

53 Born in Mendata (Bizkaia), Hormaechea was a sponsor of Basque culture and sports and a founding member and president of Euzkaldunak Incorporated Euskal Etxea (Boise).

54 Correspondence, WBFC.

55 Correspondence, WBFC.

56 Correspondence, WBFC.

57 Correspondence, WBFC.

58 Correspondence, WBFC.

59 Correspondence, WBFC.

60 WBFC.

61 Douglass, "Inventing," 141.

62 Elustondo, *Western*, 54.

63 Douglass, "Inventing," 144.

64 Rinehard, Jonathan, "The old people," WBFC.

65 Rinehard, "The old people," WBFC.

66 Rinehard, "The old people," WBFC.

67 Douglass, "Inventing," 142.

68 Camus, Argitxu. *The North American Basque Organizations (NABO), Incorporated: Ipar Amerikako Euskal Elkarteak*

1973—2007 (Gasteiz: Central Publications Service of the Basque Government, 2002), 78.

69 Correspondence, WBFC.

70 Correspondence, WBFC.

71 Correspondence, WBFC.

72 Correspondence, WBFC.

73 Correspondence, WBFC.

74 Correspondence, WBFC.

75 Correspondence, WBFC.

76 Correspondence, WBFC, translation: "to your health."

77 "Sheepmen and Biscayans," *Caldwell Tribune* (Idaho), July 17, 1909.

78 "Descendants of the Pyrenees Gather Here for Festival," *Nevada State Journal* (Reno), June 4, 1959.

Configuring One Another

My Relationship with Bob

by William A. Douglass

When I first met Bob Laxalt, in the summer of 1963, all the protagonists in this story—the people and institutions alike—were inventing themselves. The State of Nevada was less than one hundred years old, and its population was under 400,000, or just a bit more than present-day Henderson. There was no Nevada System of Higher Education; no University of Nevada, Las Vegas; and no community colleges. UNR was *the* University of Nevada. Its few thousand students were frat boys and sorority sisters, many of whom were ski bums. That summer of 1963 we feared a nuclear holocaust after the Bay of Pigs fiasco and the Cuban Missile Crisis, but a few months earlier President Kennedy was dipping his toe into what would become *our* Vietnam War.

I attended the University of Nevada from 1957 until 1961, with a parenthetical stint (1959–1960) in a New York University-sponsored junior-year-abroad program at La Complutense University in Madrid. It was there that I changed my plan of becoming a secondary school Spanish instructor to pursuing a doctorate in social anthropology.

By auditing a class in the human geography of Iberia, I had become intrigued with the possibility of one day conducting the field research for my dissertation in the Basque Country.

In short, my interest in the Basques began in Madrid and not in Reno, my hometown. When I was a child, my parents had taken me to a handful of dinners at the Basque-owned Santa Fe Hotel and to the home of their thoroughly Americanized golfing companion, Peter Echeverria. I attended Manogue High School, Northern Nevada's only parochial one. The forty students in my graduating class were in the main either Irish-American like me or Italian. I thought that my schoolmates Harvey and José Gastañaga were Italians because their surname ended in a vowel. I am uncertain if I had ever heard of the book *Sweet Promised Land*, but I had certainly never read it. I was aware of, but did not attend, the major Basque Festival in the summer of 1959 in Sparks, sponsored by the Nugget Hotel and Casino. Its owner, Dick Graves, was also a reasonably close friend of my parents, and so I had met him and his wife, Flora, on a few occasions. I was unaware that she was an Idaho Basque, as was their general manager, John Ascuaga.

Dick had visited the Basque Country with Flora and become entranced with the Basque culture and people. He was convinced that the Basque Americans should showcase their ethnic identity with a public event, so he became the driving force and underwriter of the 1959 festival. He convened a meeting of the directors of the newly formed Reno Basque club. They included both Old World-born Basques and their New World descendants. Both Ascuaga and Robert Laxalt attended, as did the flamboyant former Democratic member of the Nevada legislature, Peter Echeverria (who would eventually serve as the festival's moderator). Ironically, to generate publicity and plan the event, these organizers looked up the entry "Basques" in the *Encyclopedia Americana*. While the small group knew that Basques displayed ethnic uniqueness within the panorama of European peoples, none of the festival organizers was a scholar. In short, they needed substantive information about their language and culture to project them accurately to the wider American public.

There was also a certain ambivalence about displaying their humble rural origins as both Old World peasants and New World sheepherders. Would it evoke respect or ridicule? Basque Americans were accustomed to keeping a low profile, imbibing their ethnic personas in the intimate circles of family and friends and the semiprivate local Basque hotel. The figure of the nomadic Basque sheepman roaming the public domain of the American West, the so-called "tramp herder," had prompted a few violent confrontations with settled Anglo American ranchers. This led to "anti-Basque" legislation and litigation, in addition to negative coverage in the region's media. The Spanish-American War at the end of the nineteenth century had called into question the loyalties of Spanish Basque Americans. Then, too, there was the anti-southern European bias in the restrictive immigration legislation of the 1920s, followed by the Great Depression of the 1930s that pitted Americans against foreigners in the battered US job market. Franco's uprising in 1936 was opposed by the Basques but lauded by conservative American politicians and the hierarchy of the American Catholic Church (depicting Franco as the crusading savior of Christian civilization against the "red" threat from atheistic communism). Basque Americans kept a low profile, limiting their support of their European brethren to humanitarian aid.

By the time of the 1959 festival, there were, however, countervailing forces. The decades of interdicted Basque immigration, coupled with the manpower shortage created by the Second World War, meant that by the 1940s there was a palpable labor crisis in the sheep industry. This prompted a series of so-called "sheepherder laws" legalizing the presence of individual Basque illegal aliens who had managed to enter the country and make their way to the American West to herd sheep. US Senator Pat McCarran of Nevada, himself an ex-sheepman, championed legislation in 1950 that permitted 250 alien sheepherders into the the country. Subsequent legislation enabled the sheep ranchers' Western Range Association to employ additional herders, recruited mainly in the Spanish Basque provinces, on temporary three-year contracts.

There was also a postwar movement in the United States that began to esteem the natural environment while eulogizing rural lifestyles. The figure of the Basque herder evolved from that of the nomadic alien invader of the public lands to one of the dedicated, solitary guardians of his band in a dramatic wilderness setting. Surely, publication of *Sweet Promised Land* in 1957 provided substance to this image. The book was wildly successful and became iconic, not only of Basque immigration but of the country's immigrant heritage.

During the two years after its appearance, Laxalt had received hundreds of letters from Basque Americans throughout the American West, thanking him while noting that his family's story was that of theirs as well. This correspondence provided the festival with a mailing list of regional scope. Previously, the Bizkaian Basques of Boise, Idaho, were scarcely aware of the Navarrese and French Basque presence in Bakersfield, California. In a very real sense, *Sweet Promised Land* and what came to be called the First National Basque Festival of 1959 invented a Basque American community. In their wake, the Basques of several communities throughout the American West formed a club with its own annual summer festival—likely moderated, at least initially, by Echeverria. A festival circuit quickly developed with performers such as weightlifters and woodchoppers, as well as attendees, going from one festival to another. This growing sense of shared identity informed the founding of NABO, or North American Basque Organizations, Inc., in 1973.

As for Bill Douglass, before graduation from the University of Nevada in 1961 with a degree in Spanish language and literature, I had applied to the graduate program in social anthropology at the University of Chicago and was miraculously admitted, but without any financial aid. That first year in Chicago was extraordinarily difficult. Famed Mayanist Sol Tax made me his research assistant. He needed someone to translate from Spanish to English the extensive journals of his field assistant during their joint investigation of market relations in the Guatemalan village of Panajachel. By then, I had married Patricia Nylen, a fellow student in the Madrid program, and she was pregnant with our first child. Her father, Sven, was a building contractor in Chicago, and I worked for him both as a manual laborer and night watchman. I could do Sol's translation during my night vigilance on Sven's latest construction project in downtown Chicago.

By year's end, I was nearing burnout. I hated the Midwest and decided to apply to the University of California, Berkeley. I was accepted and given a tuition waiver. So, we moved there, and, as luck would have it, I immediately missed Chicago, or rather its university. Berkeley reminded me of the University of Nevada—large lecture classes and personal contact only with graduate assistants rather than our professors. At Chicago, our seminars were small and face-to-face with our fellow graduate students and professor. We were expected to present serious work, endure the criticisms of all, and develop the skills to critique constructively the work of others.

While on a visit to my in-laws in Chicago that Christmas, I met with Sol, and he suggested I return to Chicago. I raised the financial issue, and he proposed a solution. He would arrange for me to take my Chicago doctoral written comps off-campus in Berkeley the following May. If I passed, there would be full financial support awaiting me.

I took the two-day exams and then returned to Reno with my wife, Patricia, and our son to work construction for the summer. There was no word from Chicago. In August, I had a small windfall when a savings and loan in which my parents had gifted me stock was sold. Altogether, I now had four or five thousand dollars cash in hand, a considerable sum in those days. I could buy a new Volkswagen Beetle in Europe for $1,500. I was having considerable doubts about pursuing my career choice and decided that we should go to the Basque Country to settle in a village and commence generic field research. I had no specific topic in mind, I just wanted to *do* anthropology to determine if I was suited for it.

I had purchased the airline tickets, and we were scheduled to leave about the first of September. It was then that I got the telephone call from Fred Eggan, chairman of the Department of Anthropology at the University of Chicago, congratulating me for my high passes on the comps. I was expected back in Chicago momentarily. When I explained the situation and asked if my return could be put on hold for a year, he promised to get back to me immediately. The next day, he called to inform me that I should proceed to the Basque Country, but with my financial aid released to me while there. They would register me in courses in absentia.

It was then that I had my first encounter with Robert Laxalt. I had an older cousin, Blanche Robb, who was the assistant to Nevada's secretary of state in Carson City. When she learned of my impending sojourn in the Basque Country, she called to ask if I had discussed it with "Frenchy" Laxalt, as Bob was known in his hometown. No. Well, she would set up a meeting.

So, one late August afternoon, I went to Bob's modest home in Reno and was greeted warmly. Since we are celebrating the centennial of his birth with this conference, and I am 83, I calculate he was seventeen years my senior. Yet he, too, was in a state of transition. Before writing *Sweet Promised Land* he had been a journalist—a stringer for United Press. He regularly published stories on domestic and international affairs, but he was primarily that news service's source for Northern Nevada and California politics. Bob had parlayed the success of his book into creation of a University of Nevada Press in 1961. He was named part-time director of the nascent initiative, while also serving as the first recipient of a part-time writer-in-residence at the University. Launching the Press had been pretty much a full-time commitment, so he felt justified in spending a year in the Basque Country dedicated exclusively to his writing.

Our encounter was brief and pretty perfunctory. We did, however, agree to stay in touch to meet again in the Basque Country should we be there at the same time. I would also mention that Laxalt fame, at the time, was exclusively because of Bob. Paul Laxalt, future governor, US senator, and major figure in the Republican Party was but a small-town attorney. His sole excursion into politics had been as a single-term district attorney in Carson City. He also represented the Sparks Nugget and would eventually facilitate the transfer of its ownership from Dick Graves to John Ascuaga.

So, off we went in early September 1963 to the Basque Country. We first landed in the Navarrese village of Etxalar. It was there on a cold November evening that our landlords came to inform us that our president had been shot by an assassin.

We remained in Etxalar until the following autumn. By then, I had selected the causes and consequences of Basque emigration for my dissertation topic. I planned to reside in another village at the opposite end of the Basque Country to gain a comparative perspective. My graduate advisor at Chicago, Julian Pitt Rivers, insisted that I first spend a month or so outside the Basque Country writing up my impressions of Etxalar before confounding them with new ones from what turned out to be Aulesti, or Murelaga, in Bizkaia. So, Patricia and I had decided to travel to Austria where I would do the writeup in a quaint village that we had visited together when we were students in Madrid.

By then, Bob and his family were ensconced in St. Jean Pied de Port, or Donibane, where he was working on a new novel. Given my dissertation topic, *Sweet Promised Land* and its creator were directly relevant to my interests. So, we arranged to overnight in Donibane on our way to Austria. It was there that Bob and I had a pivotal meeting.

It seems that the Board of Regents of the University of Nevada in 1959 had approved creation of a new entity, to be named the Desert Research Institute (DRI), specializing in investigation of arid lands' environments worldwide, and in the Great Basin in particular. In 1960, academic entrepreneur Wendall Mordy was hired to launch the initiative as the DRI's first director. Although water issues and atmospheric physics were the major emphases, he envisioned a social science and humanities effort to be called the Center for Western North American Studies. Mordy convened a meeting of three prominent anthropologists, including the University of Chicago's Eggan, to advise DRI regarding the Center's research agenda. They recommended the obvious emphases on the region's paleoanthropology and prehistory as well as its contemporary Native American languages and cultures. But then, Omer Stewart of the University of Colorado proposed the creation of a Basque studies program, arguing that little was known about the Basques' contribution to Great Basin history as the region's primary sheepmen, while adding that the Basques were the "mystery people" of Europe which would provide further research opportunities.

Mordy embraced this recommendation, fully aware of the impact of *Sweet Promised Land.* Indeed, when he learned of the Laxalt family's impending sojourn in the Basque Country, he hired both Bob and his wife, Joyce, to be his emissaries. Bob's assignment was to determine if such an initiative would be accepted, and even supported, by Old World Basque academic circles. He was also to begin compiling a bibliography of

Basque-related publications (both were totally ignorant of Jon Bilbao's massive *Eusko Bibliographia* that was in progress). Joyce Laxalt was hired to take photographs of the Basque Country.

Mordy also raised the prospect of Bob becoming the first director of the Basque studies program upon his return to Reno (assuming, of course, that his investigations in the Basque Country demonstrated its feasibility). However, Bob was fully committed to his University of Nevada Press directorship and his writer-in-residency. He also felt inadequate to accept Mordy's challenge. His words to me were to the effect that: "I am not a Basque scholar, I am a Basque who writes." It was then that he asked if I would consider the position? I answered that I had yet to complete my field research, let alone write my dissertation. But after the latter, I might entertain the possibility.

Bob's report to Mordy demonstrated that a Basque studies program in Nevada would be welcomed by Old World Basques. However, the initiative would languish when the DRI was unable to find another candidate for the directorship. By early 1966, I was back in Chicago and writing my dissertation after completing my coursework. It was then that Mordy offered me the position and urged me to move to Reno immediately. In his view, I could work on my dissertation while launching the Basque studies program. I declined, suspecting that it would be like Bob's experience of trying to write while creating the University of Nevada Press. I might never finish the dissertation.

That November, I attended the annual meeting of the American Anthropological Association. Mordy's key assistant, Joy Leland, herself an anthropologist, and Warren D'Azevedo, chairman of the University of Nevada's nascent Department of Anthropology, were both there as well and encouraged me to commit to the Desert Research Institute after graduating the following summer. Although I now had offers of standard teaching posts from other universities, I was more intrigued with the challenge of continuing my Basque research while facilitating that of others. Given my dissertation topic, it was appealing to investigate what had happened in at least one strand of Basque emigration. Several families in both Etxalar and Murelaga had family in the American West.

And so, a couple of weeks after graduating from the University of Chicago in June 1967, I was driving across the United States with my father-in-law, towing a trailer filled with my professional papers and all our household belongings. My head was awash with the new challenge of launching an, as yet, indeterminate Basque studies program. Like the organizing committee of the 1959 Basque festival, we would be inventing what I would be overseeing.

In Reno, Leland and William H. Jacobsen Jr., a linguist in the English department, had submitted a proposal to the National Science Foundation for funding to create a Basque studies program that would study retention and permutation of the Basque language by Basque Americans while collecting their oral histories. It was declined. But at least I had two colleagues with whom to strategize.

Then there was Bob Laxalt. He soon informed me of the details surrounding acquisition of French Basque scholar Philippe Veyrin's personal library. Bob had discussed Nevada's Basque studies program initiative with the gravely ill intellectual, and he was so enthusiastic that he conceded to the University of Nevada the first right of refusal to purchase his personal library after his death. Bob had convinced a member of the Board of Regents, Molly Knudsen, to lend the necessary $6,000 with the condition that the debt might or might not be repaid. So, 750 Basque books were in route to Reno and would serve as the critical intellectual foundation of the Basque studies program and give it instant academic credibility. This was a major coup, since, at the time, the major research libraries in the Anglo world had at most twenty or thirty Basque-related volumes.

Bob's other interest was in creation of a Basque book series within the University of Nevada Press, edited by me. This would provide a ready publication outlet for our research.

Mordy cared little about the specific content of a Basque studies program but expected me to raise the funds for it through grants, and, unlike other DRI programs, from private donations. He was convinced that we could obtain $40,000 the first year from enthusiastic Basque Americans and eventually enough to construct our own building. That first summer, I was to go on the festival circuit to introduce the concept. As it turned out, he miscalculated the propensity of a modestly educated, rural populace to embrace such an academic endeavor. They preferred to put their efforts and resources behind their local club, in the form of its banquets, picnics, festivals, and children's folk-dance group. He also overestimated Bill Douglass's capacities as a fundraiser. Not to worry on that score, since he hired the services of a fundraiser in the University of California system to supposedly train me. While I tried, I thoroughly loathed this aspect of my job.

I had met Jon Bilbao at the same 1966 meeting of the American Anthropological Association when I committed to the DRI. Jon was a political exile from Franco's Spain and was teaching Spanish at Washington College in Maryland to earn a living. He had approached Indiana University, Vassar College, and the American Museum of Natural History in New York with proposals to start a Basque studies program, but without success. He was delighted by DRI's initiative and the acquisition of the Veyrin collection. He offered his assistance.

In the spring of 1968, I secured the funding to pay Jon's travel expenses to Reno to give a public lecture on the Basque language. An overflow crowd attended. That week, Jon and I brainstormed about possible initiatives for the Basque Studies Program. He was a fount of ideas. He offered to microfilm during the following summer for our Basque library collection some unique critical documents regarding Basque nationalism housed in the French Basque Country if I could secure the necessary funding. I did so with a single call to the director of the library. Jon subsequently told me that that was what convinced him that the University of Nevada was the real deal.

As I neared the end of my first year, I was unhappy being Mordy's huckster and of being a one-person Basque Studies Program. I told him I was leaving. Mordy asked what it would take for me to stay, and I answered that I would if he hired Jon Bilbao. Jon relinquished his tenure-track position at Washington College for the offer of a one-year contract at DRI and the chance to pursue his dream. Meanwhile, I received grant funds for a study of ethnicity maintenance among Basque Americans. Between that and Jon's ongoing bibliographic research, the Basque Studies Program now had an actual research agenda. We also began teaching classes at the University of Nevada—Jon was the Basque language instructor, and I gave a course in Old World Basque culture.

Bob Laxalt maintained a curious relationship with the Basque Studies Program and me. Like with the securing of the Veyrin collection, he was always there to help when asked. The same year of 1967 that I became head of the Basque Studies Program, Paul Laxalt became the governor of Nevada. Bob had been totally involved in the campaign, including writing some of Paul's speeches.

Bob now convinced Paul to host a dinner in the Governor's Mansion for potential Basque Studies Program donors. At Bob's behest, Paul subsequently included funding for Jon Bilbao's position in his budgetary request. Then, too, when it was decided to move the Basque Studies Program from DRI to the University of Nevada, Reno, in the late 1970s, Bob used his influence in the Nevada Legislature, and particularly with the longtime senator Bill Raggio, to secure funding for our operating budget. When Jon retired in 1980 and returned to the Basque Country, Bob lobbied the legislature successfully for a part-time Basque librarian position, as he did when we requested a new professional position for me.

While he was our loyal proponent, Bob took no interest in the day-to-day operations of the Basque Studies Program. In part, there was the physical distance. Our offices were at the former Stead Air Force Base, about eight miles from his on the Reno campus. However, the Basque collection had two rooms in the basement of the Getchell Library, a short stroll across the quad from Bob's office. Bilbao spent his afternoons and evenings there doing his bibliographic research and serving as the de facto Basque librarian. I was there frequently as well, both conferring with Jon and reading the books. Yet I am not sure that Bob ever entered our physical premises more than the one time when he accompanied Paul on the governor's own sole visit to the Basque Studies Program.

This is not to say that Bob and I were distant. Indeed, the opposite was true. We began to have lunch regularly, every three weeks or so, and we became confidantes. He knew that my politics were liberal, and he liked to try ideas out on me that he was incorporating into his speechwriting for Paul. Office politics at the University of Nevada Press were often complicated and even nasty, so, on several occasions, Bob sought my advice. Through my involvement in my family's casinos, I had business experience. Bob regularly asked me for financial counsel, and, on one occasion, we almost entered into a real estate investment together. We also collaborated closely on the project to erect in Reno's Rancho San Rafael Park the National Monument to the Basque Sheepherder.

And then there was the writing. In my capacity as Basque Book Series editor, I was an ex-officio member of his editorial board. So, in addition to Basque books, I was evaluating submissions that largely regarded the American West, and particularly Nevada. My training in seminars at Chicago had honed my critical skills. So, from the outset, Bob asked me to edit his first drafts.

Except for *Sweet Promised Land*, I believe that I did a preliminary edit (both copy and stylistic) of every one of his books. With rare exceptions, he accepted and incorporated my suggestions.

Regarding the Basque Book Series, Bob deferred to my acquisition decisions. We began the series with a reprint of Rodney Gallop's classic *A Book of the Basques*, long since out-of-print. It was a huge success and was sold out in a few weeks. Bob had submitted what became our second title, *In a Hundred Graves*, regarding it to be his one obligatory contribution to a series that was, after all, his idea. I envisioned further reprints in translation of two other classics—Philippe Veyrin's *Les Basques* and Julio Caro Baroja's *Los Vascos*. But, by then, we were overwhelmed with submissions of original works.

I therefore abandoned the idea of reprints, but with one exception—*Sweet Promised Land*. It, too, was long since out-of-print. But then, to my chagrin, Bob acceded when Paul's closely contested campaign in 1974 to become one of Nevada's US senators asked him to write a rather cloying introduction to a reprint of *Sweet Promised Land* that was then distributed gratis as pro-Laxalt political propaganda. Indeed, Bob and I had probably our strongest disagreement over what I thought to be crass exploitation of his iconic classic.

Bob retired as director of the University of Nevada Press in 1983 to dedicate himself entirely to his writing. We remained close—continuing our regular lunch dates (now often in Carson City because he was living at the southern end of Washoe Valley). I still felt that a proper reprint of *Sweet Promised Land* was a natural for the Basque Book Series. However, whenever I raised the possibility with Bob, he demurred. His agent opposed the idea since they had had feelers from Hollywood for a possible film contract. Should there be a movie, there would obviously be demand for a reprint of the book from a commercial publisher. An even more important factor was Bob's reticence to be perceived as self-serving. He was concerned how people would interpret publication of him by him as former director of the University of Nevada Press.

Our little tug-of-war continued until I convinced him to submit a novella, *A Cup of Tea in Pamplona* (1985), to the series after his agent failed to place it commercially. Well and good, but there remained my desire to reprint his opus magnus. While he no longer dreamed of the film possibility, he continued to worry about the perception of self service should the Press publish the book. So finally, I said something to the effect that "it isn't your decision to reprint *Sweet Promised Land* in the Basque Book Series, it's mine." He went along and even acceded, somewhat reluctantly, to my offer to write an introduction to the new edition. He felt that the book should stand on its own. While we never discussed the matter, I intended my introduction as a palliative to the one he had written for Paul's campaign. Bob's dedication of my copy states, "For my dear friend Bill Douglass. Who saw with so much perception—more than I—what this book really meant."

Sweet Promised Land was reprinted in the Basque Book Series in 1986 and became an instant bestseller. I believe that it has sold more copies than any other title ever published by the University of Nevada Press. The floodgate was now open. Bob quickly submitted the first volume, *The Basque Hotel* (1989), of what he conceived to be his Basque trilogy, again when his agent failed to find a commercial publisher in advance. Obviously, the subsequent two volumes, *The Child of the Holy Ghost* (1992) and *The Governor's Mansion* (1994), would logically come out in the same venue.

Meanwhile, we published *A Time We Knew: Images of Yesterday in the Basque Homeland* (1990). I was, of course, aware of Bob's earlier articles regarding the Basque Country in *National Geographic* magazine. He had collaborated with renowned photographer, William Allard. The Basque Country had changed radically since the articles (hence the title of the new volume), and I now encouraged Bob to contact Allard for permission to produce a work employing his text and the photographer's images.

Throughout the remainder of his retirement, Bob published all his subsequent books with the Press. With one exception, *The Land of My Fathers: A Son's Return to the Basque Country* (1999), none was particularly Basque-related and so did not appear in the Basque Book Series. My only relation to them was to continue providing Bob with a reading of his first draft. I, too, retired from my position from UNR on December 31, 1999. While I continued to edit the Basque Book Series for a few years until some in-progress book projects were completed, I then vacated that position as well.

If Bob had been instrumental in securing my legacy by helping to facilitate transfer of the Basque Studies Program to UNR, along with securing funding for my position, I was able to salvage his. After his retirement, the University of Nevada Press began running a serious annual deficit to the degree that my good friend, Mark Dawson, then chancellor of the Nevada System of Higher Education, informed me that he was planning to abolish it. I prevailed upon him to give us one last chance. He agreed on the condition that I, and two other Press board members whom he respected, would assume oversight of the Press's finances. For about the next two years, we worked closely with the Press's director, approving (or not) all proposed expenditures.

Such, then, is an overview of my personal history with Robert Laxalt. We were collaborators rather than colleagues in the strictest sense. While Jon Bilbao and I developed a relationship that was similarly as intimate as it was professional, I was always his supervisor. So many of our exchanges were obligatory rather than consensual. The opposite was true for Bob and me. We sought out one another's company. I wouldn't say that we were one another's "best friend," however, as reflected in the title of this chapter, it is my belief that neither of us would have been the person we became had we never met.

Robert Laxalt 100th Birthday Conference, March 10, 2023

Good afternoon—My name is Gabriel Urza, and I am one of Robert Laxalt's four grandchildren.

I want to start off, on behalf of the Laxalt family, by expressing our profound gratitude to all the people and institutions that have made these two days a reality: Iñaki Arrieta Baro, Xabier Irujo, the Center for Basque Studies, the University of Nevada Press, David Rio, and Bill Douglass, and all the other presenters and panelists who have spoken here.

It's difficult to articulate what it means to have the work of Robert—our father, our grandfather, someone we loved so much—continue to be discussed and recognized in this way. When I talk to someone who has read his work—*Sweet Promised Land*, or *In a Hundred Graves*—I often have the feeling that a part of my grandfather is still alive. That he is still present in the room with us. I've had that sensation so many times in the last two days.

I've been thinking a lot about what my grandfather would say if he were here today. Chances are, he'd be as nervous as I am now to talk in front of you all. But I know also how happy he would be to know that we are still reading and engaging in his work.

People often talk about books as a form of immortality, that the author gets to live on after their death. But books like *Sweet Promised Land* aren't just monuments to their authors;

they are about the memories and collective experiences of the people who live inside of them, the people whom they are about. Over the years, I often meet people—first-generation Basques, but immigrants from many places—who feel like the stories of *their* families are immortalized in these books.

Robert's writing isn't just about the cultures we leave behind to come to the US, but also the sense of estrangement, and displacement, that children of immigrants often feel. The sensation of being trapped between cultures. The question of what you're entitled to have an opinion on, or a voice about. And I think that's what often resonates so deeply with people—that sense, as David Rio said yesterday—of simultaneously being an insider and an outsider.

*

I grew up on College Drive, right across the street from the University of Nevada, Reno. I have such vivid memories of coming to the university to see my grandfather, whether he was speaking at the Getchell Library or the old bookstore or working at his office at the Press. So many of the people whom I see here in the audience today are the same people that fill my earliest memories, and coming back here today feels like time travel—we are all older. Good and bad things have happened since then. We've grown up. But when we gather here to talk about Robert's work, I feel transported back to those early days.

One of the things I've come to appreciate most about growing up near Robert Laxalt was that I got to know him as a grandfather first, and an author second. He was rarely this person we see in the photographs or read about in articles or biographies, on horseback in Argentina or in a den of spies in the Belgian Congo. He wasn't even the person who had written all the incredible books that we've been talking about in the last two days. Instead, he was just Tatchi to us—he was the grandfather who liked to mow his pasture on an old Sears riding mower, who bullshitted us with a story of seeing a gold nugget in the creek just to keep the grandkids looking for hours. He was the grandfather who lifted you up to play the slot machine at the Santa Fe, or who let you try on his old black boxing gloves.

I learned from him that writers are human. I learned that my grandfather had a fear of public speaking, that even after a lifetime of writing there was still a palpable anxiety when he was working on a book. I still remember the unspoken religious ceremony that would take place when a manuscript was completed: the family would all arrive for our usual visit to my grandparents' house in Washoe Valley, and there on a silver serving platter on a table in the entryway would be a manilla envelope with the completed manuscript inside. It was sort of like when the Vatican sends up the smoke when they've elected a new pope.

*

Some of you might remember my grandfather driving around town in his old International Scout—he drove that truck for thirty years, and I don't think he ever figured out where the blinker switch was. Every time he went around a corner, he'd accidentally turn on the windshield wipers.

That truck's been sitting outside my mom's house for the last twenty years. The Scout has one of those smells that instantly transports you into memory—and every time I open the door, I remember the first time I ever drove a car, this car, with my dad, Carmelo, and with Tatchi out on the Black Rock desert when I was about ten.

I was poking around in the back of the Scout one afternoon, maybe a decade after he died, and I found this leather bag stashed in a wooden box in the back, under an old sleeping bag and next to a flashlight, a candle, and matches. (He always had these survival supplies on hand, and I think one of the great regrets of his life was never getting stuck overnight in a blizzard in the Scout).

Without really thinking about it, I grabbed the bag and have kept it ever since. A few weeks ago, in preparation for this conference, I finally opened the bag and started to sort through the contents. The first thing I found was this—twenty-five single-space pages of notes that he had taken while on assignment for *National Geographic* in Argentina—full pages of descriptions of what the gauchos were wearing, what they ate, how they moved, how their animals ate and moved. You can see all the work that went into a one- or two-line description in the final article, how he distilled these complex lives into simple, three-dimensional images. You can see all the work it takes to write so little but say so much.

The second thing in the bag is the manuscript for *The Governor's Mansion*, the last book in the Basque trilogy. If you haven't read it, *The Governor's* Mansion is a biographical novel about Robert's brother, Paul's, election as lieutenant governor in 1962. I was so glad to see David discuss this book yesterday—it's a novel that doesn't get much attention, but it feels so prescient in its discussion about how power works in Nevada, and more broadly in the United States. As David points out, it's also a novel about loss—about how fulfilling the American Dream, making it in politics and in broader American life, often comes at the cost of our own identities.

I've spent the last week reading the book in its early draft form—I can see my grandfather's handwritten notes in the margins, I can see four different rewrites of a single chapter. But mostly, I feel like I'm watching him make sense of his own life, and that of his family. I can see him tally the cost of success and power and corruption in his own family, and struggle to balance how much of his complicated feelings about his brother's life in politics to commit to paper. As he writes in the novel, after the narrator's brother is elected:

For Leon, it meant that he had been elected governor of a state. For his campaign workers, it meant victory against overwhelming odds. For my mother, it meant loss, regardless of Leon's assurance. For my father, it meant confusion and dismay and flight into the mountains. For me, election night was a harbinger of things to come. It was the night when the treasured privacy of our family home was invaded and violated permanently.

I have kept these pages for the past ten years—and as I've carried them, I've felt like I've been carrying my grandfather with me. But I think they belong here, with the university and with all of you, and so we will donate them to the Robert Laxalt Papers collection here at UNR. I think nothing would make my grandfather happier than to have them here, with you.

On behalf of my family, thanks again to everyone who participated in this conference, and who attended, and who continues to read Robert Laxalt's work.

About the Authors

IÑAKI ARRIETA BARO is the head of the Jon Bilbao Basque Library, a highly specialized unit focused on serving researchers from all around the world interested in Basque Studies. He leads the planning, promotion, advocacy, and policy development efforts for the Basque Library. In collaboration with other librarians and faculty from other departments, he has taken part in the organization of workshops and conferences in connections with Basque topics and digital humanities. Iñaki works with both local researchers and scholars worldwide, collaborates with the Basque American community on preservation efforts of documents in different physical forms and digital assets, and works with donors in obtaining new materials for our Basque collections.

WILLIAM A. DOUGLASS was born in Reno, Nevada. He received his BA from the University of Nevada in Spanish Literature in 1961, then earned his MS in 1966, and then PhD from the University of Chicago in Anthropology in 1967. He also attended the University of Madrid from 1959-60, the University of Oslo in 1960, and UC Berkeley from 1962-3. In 1967, he joined the Anthropology faculty at UNR and founded the Basque Studies Program, now known as the Center for Basque Studies. He was its first director and served in that capacity for 33 years.

XABIER IRUJO is professor of genocide studies for the Center for Basque Studies at the University of Nevada, Reno. He was the first guest research scholar of the Manuel Irujo Chair at the University of Liverpool and has taught seminars on genocide and cultural genocide at Boise State University in Idaho, and at the University of California, Santa Barbara. He holds three master's degrees in linguistics, history, and philosophy and has two PhDs in history and philosophy. Dr. Irujo has lectured in nearly one hundred American and European universities and academic or cultural institutions. He has published on issues related to Basque history and politics and has specialized throughout his career in genocide studies with a focus on physical and cultural extermination. Dr. Irujo has authored more than fifteen books and a number of articles in specialized journals and has received awards and honors at a national and international level. His recent books include *Gernika: Genealogy of a Lie* (Sussex Academic Press, 2018), *"Arrasaré Vizcaya". 2000 bombardeos aéreos en Euskadi* (University of the Basque Country Press, 2020), and *Legal History of the Basque Language* (HAEE, Bilbao, 2015).

MONIQUE LAXALT is the daughter of Robert Laxalt. She was born and raised in Reno, Nevada, except for 2 years when her family was living in the French-Basque Country. She received her B.A. in English Literature from Stanford University, and her M.A. in French Literature and Juris Doctorate from the University of Iowa. She practiced law in Reno for 36 years before recently retiring. Laxalt and her former husband Carmelo Urza raised two children together: Gabriel Urza and Alexandra Urza, who spent time in the Basque Country during their childhoods, adolescence, and young adulthood.

WARREN LERUDE is a veteran American journalist and consultant to global publishing, academic, judicial, and legislative organizations. Lerude led a team of three journalists to win the Pulitzer Prize for Editorial Writing in 1977 as executive editor of the *Reno Evening Gazette* and *Nevada State Journal* where he also served as publisher. Lerude is author of the biography *Robert Laxalt, The Story of a Story Teller,* published by the Center for Basque Studies Press in 2013. He was instrumental in the development of the Reynolds School of Journalism at the University of Nevada, Reno, where he taught media law and management and administered the professional internship program for thirty years. Lerude and Robert Laxalt were close friends and colleagues in journalism, teaching, and publishing.

MONIKA MADINABEITIA is an associate professor at the Faculty of Humanities and Education Sciences (Mondragon University). She is currently the co-coordinator of the recently launched degree Global Digital Humanities, which is located in Zorrotzaurre, Bilbao. She published the illustrated book *Petra, My Basque Grandmother* in 2018. Her main research areas are identity and e/migration, with an emphasis on the Basque American diaspora in the US West. Her teaching mainly focuses on culture and identity. She has been teaching Basque Culture to international students since 2007 and has participated in different courses and lectures held by Etxepare Institute.

SANDRA OTT is Professor of Anthropology at the University of Nevada, Reno. She works at the intersections of cultural history and anthropology in her research on the German Occupation of Iparralde and Béarn, Basque resistance movements, the postwar trials of suspected collaborators, and the experiences of Jews. Her current book project focuses on the wartime and postwar journeys of Jews in the Basque borderlands and beyond.

DAVID RIO is Professor of American Literature at the University of the Basque Country (EHU) in Vitoria-Gasteiz. His research interests are located within the field of American Studies, with an emphasis on diaspora studies, regional literatures, and especially western American writing and Basque-American literature. He is the author of *El proceso de la violencia en la narrativa de Robert Penn Warren* (1995), *Robert Laxalt: The Voice of the Basques in American Literature* (2007), and *New Literary Portraits of the American West: Contemporary Nevada Fiction* (2014). He has co-edited six volumes on the literature of the American West, the special issue of the journal *Western American Literature* on "Writing the Global Western" (2019), and *The Western in the Global Literary Imagination* (2022). He has also edited *La expansión y revisión de un mito: el Oeste norteamericano en la literatura española* (2023). David Rio coordinates an international research group (REWEST) specialized in the literature and culture of the American West.

GRETCHEN SKIVINGTON is emerita professor of humanities at Great Basin College in Elko, Nevada. Her Basque immigrant grandparents built Elko's first Basque hotel, The Overland, in 1908. Her Nevada novel *Echevarria* was greatly influenced by the American Basque themes of the works of Robert Laxalt whom she met and conferred with on various occasions in the 1980s. Like Bob Laxalt, she was the recipient of a Fulbright fellowship and has been recognized by the Nevada Arts Council and the Rockefeller Foundation as a fiction fellow. She has published articles in historical journals including *Halcyon* and the *Northeastern Nevada Historical Society Quarterly*. Her novel *Echevarria,* based on Elko's Overland Hotel, was highlighted at the National Cowboy Poetry Gathering "Basques & Buckaroos" in Elko, Nevada in 2018. She lives in Elko and is finishing the second novel *Barria* of her own Basque-hotel trilogy *Echevarria.*

GABRIEL URZA is a member of the creative writing faculty at Portland State University whose work has appeared in *The New York Times*, *The Guardian*, *Salon Magazine*, *Slate*, *Politico*, and elsewhere. His first novel, *All That Followed*, was published by Henry Holt & Co. in 2015 and was a *New York Times* Editor's Choice. He is also the recipient of the Miriam Shearing Fellowship at the Black Mountain Institute and was a 2022 Fulbright Scholar. Prior to pursuing an MFA in Creative Writing at Ohio State University, he worked for five years as a public defender in Reno, Nevada.

MARIANN VACZI is an Associate Professor of Anthropology at the University of Nevada, Reno. As an ethnographer, she works at the intersections of sport, politics, culture, and society. Her main work includes *Catalonia's Human Towers: Castells, Cultural Politics, and the Struggle Toward the Heights* (Indiana University Press, 2023), *Soccer, Culture, and Society in Spain: An Ethnography of Basque Fandom* (Routledge 2015), *Indigenous, Traditional, and Folk Sports: Contesting Modernities* (co-edited with Alan Bairner, Routledge 2024), and *Sport and Secessionism* (co-edited with Alan Bairner, Routledge 2021).

Index

Note: End note information is indicated by n and note number following the page number.

www.ingramcontent.com/pod-product-compliance
Lightning Source LLC
LaVergne TN
LVHW020719110826
845149LV00012B/2332

* 9 7 8 1 9 6 7 1 7 9 1 0 7 *